D0283112

Dangerous Devotions for Guys

DARE TO LIVE YOUR FAITH

Incredible things will happen™

Loveland, Colorado
group.com

Group resources really work!

This Group resource incorporates our R.E.A.L. approach to ministry. It reinforces a growing friendship with Jesus, encourages long-term learning, and results in life transformation, because it's

Relational
Learner-to-learner interaction enhances learning and builds Christian friendships.

Experiential
What learners experience through discussion and action sticks with them up to 9 times longer than what they simply hear or read.

Applicable
The aim of Christian education is to equip learners to be both hearers and doers of God's Word.

Learner-based
Learners understand and retain more when the learning process takes into consideration how they learn best.

Dangerous Devotions for Guys
Dare to Live Your Faith

Copyright © 2009 Tim Shoemaker
Visit our website: **group.com**

Credits
Author: Tim Shoemaker
Executive Developer: Amy Nappa
Chief Creative Officer: Joani Schultz
Assistant Editor: Daniel Birks
Cover Art Director/Designer and Art Director: Jeff A. Storm
Book Designer and Print Production Artist: Bob Bubnis
Production Manager: DeAnne Lear

Library of Congress Cataloging-in-Publication Data
Shoemaker, Tim.
 Dangerous devotions for guys : dare to live your faith / Tim Shoemaker. — 1st American pbk. ed.
  p. cm.
 ISBN 978-0-7644-3734-2 (pbk. : alk. paper) 1. Church work with teenagers. 2. Teenage boys. I. Title.
 BV4447.S56 2008
 259'.23—dc22
                    2008009122

10 9 8 7 6 5 4 3   17 16 15 14 13 12
Printed in the United States of America.

NOTICE!

This book contains a number of activities that may be dangerous. All of these activities should be carried out under adult supervision only. The author and publishers expressly disclaim liability for any injury or damages that result from engaging in the activities contained in this book.

● DEDICATION

To the memory of Gabriel Skrudland and Vaughn Shoemaker—two men who prayed for their grandson and left behind the heritage of an example to follow.

To my sons, Andy, Mark, and Luke. Your lives keep me on my toes.

To my wife, Cheryl. Your love keeps me on my knees.

Most important, to my Lord. Your grace keeps me on my feet.

● ACKNOWLEDGMENTS

To Marlene Bagnull and Nancy Rue—for their time, love, encouragement, and mentoring

To Brian Davis, Cec Murphey, and Michael Dellosso—for their friendship, encouragement, and prayers

To Rob, Shawn, Andy, and Mark—for reviewing my ideas and brainstorming with me

To Luke—for testing object lessons with me, especially the ones with fire

To my senior high small group—for being wonderful guinea pigs

To Dr. Dan Varnell—for the "puking pumpkin" formula

To Jim Winchell—for helping in a way he may not even remember

To Amy Nappa, Rick Lawrence, and the good crew at Group—for their vision and for giving me the nod

To Dr. Dale McElhinney, Pam Halter, Joyce Moccero, Dawn Moore, Candy Abbott, and the rest of the "Crue" for their friendship and inspiration

To Dad and Mom—for undying support, unwavering confidence, unconditional love, and unselfish wisdom

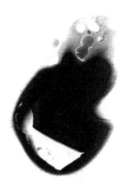

| The first fire department began in 1860, when the Hook and Ladder Company No. 1 held an
organizational meeting on April 6, 1860. |

Table of Contents

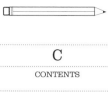

This isn't quite like other small group books you may have used. To maximize your effectiveness, read the **Introduction** section first. It reveals the *best secrets I know* to leading a powerful small group or devotional time for guys. Everything in this book hinges on those factors. And the **How to Use This Book** section has additional info that is *vital.* Don't skip it! After that, choose activities in any order that you like.

Introduction 7
Tired of "Safe" Devotions for Guys?

How to Use This Book 9
The Most Dangerous Thing You Can Do...
Is Skip This Section

American Graffiti 11
Sheets of drywall and cans of spray paint will offer the guys a chance to leave their "mark" with a little graffiti fun. This will lead the guys to look at the kind of mark they're making in life and to discover whether God really has a plan or purpose for them.

Bag Lunch 16
Mixing seemingly random things in a plastic bag and boiling them in water will get a discussion cooking about how God blends things together in our lives to make something good.

Hot Stuff 21
Tossing a handful of nondairy creamer into a raging campfire will create a burst of flame that will bring a smile to any guy's face. This will fuel a discussion about the destructive risks guys take and using that gutsy energy to do constructive things for God.

Get More From Less 27
A squirt-gun fight to the finish opens the door to talk about dissatisfaction with the hand God has dealt us in life.

Boating or Floating? 33
A very wet canoe ride will show how we'll eventually sink if we compromise the values and principles God has given us to live by.

Micro-Mess 37
Exploding an egg in the microwave exposes the truth that hidden sin in our life will change us on the inside and make a real mess.

Watch Your Step 41
A rat-trap maze will lead guys to understand the need to avoid traps in life while encouraging others to do the same.

Easy Target 47
A fire and squirt guns will highlight the importance of Christian community.

Get a Grip 53
An easy task becomes nearly impossible as we illustrate the importance of living a "clean" life.

Fountain of Truth 57
A geyser of Diet Coke will help teach the truth about anger and the sticky problems it creates.

Puking Pumpkin 63
White lies, half-truths, and whoppers. We'll use a little chemistry lesson and a jack-o'-lantern to make the point that when we tell one lie, a whole lot more gush out to follow it.

Sack of Potatoes   69
A little exercise with potatoes will underscore the absolute need to forgive others.

Sack of Potatoes 2   74
In this sequel from last week, the potatoes are getting old, heavy, and are perfect for illustrating the downside of failing to forgive others.

Flamethrower   79
Making a flamethrower may be fun, but it wouldn't be a smart thing to teach younger kids. This blazes a trail to talk about our responsibility to be a good example to others.

Steel Penny Christians   85
A handful of World War II steel pennies and a strong magnet will pull the guys into a discussion about living like Christians even when nobody is looking.

Gravity and Other Guarantees   91
Using water balloons to illustrate the law of gravity will also launch a discussion about another absolute principle— honoring our parents is something God expects and rewards.

Wrecking Yard   96
Looking at cars that have been totaled or badly damaged will tow you right into a talk about how letting down our guard can put our life on the scrapheap, too, especially after we head off to college.

The Right Combination   101
You'll challenge guys to open combination locks—without the right combination. The fact that only one sequence of numbers can unlock each lock will open a discussion about absolute truth and unlocking the truth of God's Word.

Defective Perspective   107
We'll use a variety of items to explore the need to seek perspectives other than our own.

The Three-legged Race Case   112
Running an obstacle course tied to another guy is tough, but when you make each of them face opposite directions, it's insane. This will get you off and running on a talk about the dangers of dating a non-Christian.

Beauty Is a Beast   117
A trip to a used car lot to pick a dream car or truck fast-lanes you into a talk about choosing a date based on her heart—not just on her looks.

Lethal Lure   122
A tackle box "lure tour" will lead to a discussion about the fact that the devil and his demons are excellent fishermen who are intent on setting their hooks in us. We'll look at the subtleness of temptation and the results of taking the bait.

Fireproof   127
We'll mix and test a solution that actually makes cloth flame retardant. This will spark a discussion about how to prepare so we avoid getting "burned" by temptation.

Sugar Substitute   133
Demonstrating an easy yet impressive chemical reaction will blaze a trail for a talk about the devastating effects that viewing pornography now can have on truly great sex after marriage.

Introduction

Tired of "Safe" Devotions for Guys?

Ever feel like you're not getting anywhere with your guys small group? You spend time finding just the right book and give each of them a copy. After two or three weeks it's obvious the only one reading the book is you. Not exactly great for discussion—or discipleship.

This traditional small group model—giving the guys a book—is widely accepted. It's *safe.* Too bad it doesn't always work for junior high or high school guys.

Maybe It's Time to Change the Model

This book features the technique Jesus used when he taught *his* small group of disciples. He didn't ask them to read a scroll and come back a week later to discuss it. Jesus taught *visually*—and with amazing and unexpected results. He used inventive object lessons. Water into wine, the coin found in a fish's mouth, walking on water, calming the storm, and the withering fig tree.

Think of all the accounts of the diseased, the lame, and the blind. Again and again the disciples observed the sick and watched Jesus heal. Often *this* is how he taught them about his love, his power, and true faith. When the time came to teach his last and most important lesson, he used an object lesson again—the cross. He taught us about sacrificial love and forgiveness.

This book is going to take that object lesson approach to your devotional time, by involving every guy in the process. Guys won't just *watch* you do something cool—they'll be doing it *with* you, experiencing everything for themselves, and then discovering how what they're doing applies in their own lives.

Jesus didn't play it safe—and we're going to follow his lead. So you won't be giving the guys another book that they won't read. This book is for you alone. Each week you'll lead a devotional activity that will get guys' attention and naturally lead into a discussion about a principle God has given us to live by.

Three More Secrets You Don't Want to Risk Missing

The Food Factor—Jesus knew all about the effectiveness of incorporating food for the stomach with food for the soul. He did it so often that his critics called him a glutton. Jesus turned mealtimes into milestones. The Last Supper, for example. And how about the life-changing "Do you love me?" exchange with Peter after Jesus made breakfast for his disciples in John 21? Remember the account in Luke 7 about the woman who washed Jesus' feet with her tears? Jesus used it to teach a great lesson, and yes, he was at the dinner table.

I've been doing this with the small group of high school seniors my wife and I lead. I'm amazed at the difference food makes. After the devotion we serve real food, and plenty of it. I'm not talking snacks. We serve things like sloppy Joes, tacos, hot dogs, pancakes, pizza, and lasagna. Something different every week. We serve them dessert, too.

We start with the activity, and then the guys eat *while* we discuss it. Guys feel more comfortable while they're eating, and it also gives them something to do with their hands. If you can't bring the food to the guys, bring the guys to the food and hit a fast-food restaurant together.

Don't underestimate the difference you'll make by consistently serving good food. They'll love it—and they'll *listen*.

The Benefits Factor—The Bible is our authority—*but that's not necessarily the case for all of your guys.* You've read the same scary statistics I've read. Teenagers and young adults don't simply accept everything the Bible says as the final truth anymore.

I talked to a carload of students recently about this book. One of them mentioned how he hates it when leaders don't go any further than the Bible when telling them how they should or shouldn't be living. The teaching comes across as negative—as "do's and don'ts." The other students agreed. The lesson I got out of that conversation was this: Tell them what the Bible says, but also explain why it makes good *sense* to do it God's way. The benefits to them are generally huge—but we need to help them see it. And never fail to let them know you *do* believe in the authority of the Bible. Your example means more than you'll ever know.

The Love Factor—This is essential for leading effective small group devotions. You need to *care.* You need to love these guys. Ask God to give you a heart for them. Of all the tips I've tried to highlight in this book, the greatest of these is love.

A Few More Tips—

Confidentiality: This might seem like common sense to you, but be sure you set up an environment that is also emotionally safe for the guys. Agree with them that what's shared at group stays at group.

Group size: These devotions work great for a small group of guys. How small? Probably about the number of guys you can fit into your own living room. These are going to have a lot more impact if you're in a comfortable setting such as a home, and keeping the group smaller ensures that every guy gets a chance to participate and to talk during the discussion. It also helps keep your costs for supplies down. If you have more guys coming than you can handle, recruit a friend to lead with you for a few weeks, and then have him take a few of the guys and start a new group. Expand!

Discussion: I've provided a lot of discussion questions with each devotion. Really let the guys dig into talking. Encourage them to tell about their own lives. Don't rush through the questions. It's OK if guys need a few minutes to think about what you've asked. Just because no one talks immediately doesn't mean they're not thinking. A few moments of silence are OK. And as time goes by and the guys are more comfortable and trusting of you and each other, they'll be more willing to open up.

Dads: This is a great book to use if you're a dad with a son (or several sons). Gather your boys and some of their friends to do these devotions. Get another dad on board with you. These are excellent ways to get involved in the spiritual development of your young men—and have fun together, too!

Use your Bible: Let the guys in your group see you opening your Bible and reading the passages I've included with each devotion. It's a great example for them and shows them that you're not making this stuff up—it comes directly from God's Word.

Tired of "safe" small group sessions? So are your guys.

They're ready for something different. Dangerous. Let's follow Jesus' pattern. He knew how to get through to guys...*and his small group changed the world.*

HOW TO USE THIS BOOK

The Most Dangerous Thing You Can Do...*Is Skip This Section* (Or, How to Avoid Plastic Surgery)

- **Safety Issues**—It probably hasn't escaped your notice that the title of this book includes the word *Dangerous.* Some of these sessions do require the use of chemicals, combustible materials, fire, and all kinds of things that guys will love. Promise me you'll exercise good judgment when it comes to safety. Visuals are great, but not when they end up in someone's eye. Use gloves, goggles, and common sense all the way—or we won't come out with *More Dangerous Devotions for Guys.* Deal?

GOGGLE ZONE

You'll notice a "Danger Level" icon at the beginning of each activity. This icon lets you know at a glance whether the activity is low, medium, or high risk when it comes to safety. Take every precaution to make sure that every guy will have the safety equipment needed to keep eyes, fingers, and all other body parts intact.

RISK

LOW   MED   HI

- **Prep in Advance**—All of these sessions will go better if you read them a week or so in advance so your mind can be working on it. In most cases there will be supplies to track down and pick up—so don't wait until the last minute. The guys will sense if you're throwing it together at the last second, and they'll have a hard time respecting that. Want to maximize your impact with the guys? Put in the prep time.

- **Practice Ahead of Time**—Resist the urge to shortcut the lesson in some way. Otherwise, you may cut short the *effectiveness* of the session while you're at it. And because you want each session to start strong, always practice the activity *before* you try it with the guys. No matter how easy it seems, you'll always learn something when you test it. That little bit of extra experience will make your small group time just a touch better.

- **Coaching Tips**—Consider most of the text in brown print as coaching tips written just for you. The text in orange print represents things you say to the guys or ask them. You can adapt these sections in bold print to your own voice. It's important to speak the way you normally speak or you'll come across as being fake or scripted—and that will affect the way the guys respond.

- **Drive Home the Point, but Don't Run Them Over**—Keep the teaching time short. The guys aren't stupid. They'll get your point, so don't risk boring them. The guys will get more out of the session if they're actively involved in discussion instead of just listening to you.

- **Pack a Digital Camera**—This is a key element. Shoot pictures during each activity—or appoint one of the guys as your official group photographer and let him use your camera. Everybody looks for themselves in pictures, and you don't want anyone disappointed. You'll use these pictures later as a reminder to the guys of the small group session theme.

- **Sending an E-mail**—A few days after your small group time, send out a blanket e-mail to each of the guys with a brief reminder of the session and attach some of the pictures you took. This is a foundational reinforcement strategy. You'll use this to encourage them to apply what they learned during small group time to their everyday lives—and they'll look forward to seeing themselves in the pictures.

- **Takeaways**—Some sessions will recommend you give each of the guys something that ties in with the theme or activity somehow. It's all about keeping the truth of your session in front of them during the week and beyond, so this is really important.

Ready to get started? Grab your safety goggles and let's go!

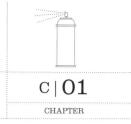

THEME
Leave your "mark" in life by accomplishing God's plans for you.

TITLE

C | 01
CHAPTER

American Graffiti

● PREP

Because of the obvious mess and paint fumes, find a good spot outdoors to do this. This is one of those rare activities where you don't need to practice in advance.

RISK

| LOW | MED | HI |

● GETTING STARTED

When you get together with the guys, spread out the plastic, if needed, and line up the plywood or paneling against a wall, fence, or other sturdy object. Give each guy a can of spray paint, and explain that you'd like them to take 10 minutes to "leave their mark" on the plywood. They can write their name, include a statement (in good taste), or spray-paint a picture or symbol that expresses who they are. If you bought an array of spray paint colors, suggest the guys trade cans for variety.

Don't be surprised if they leave their "mark" on each other. If that's the case, roll with it. If you're concerned about this ahead of time, you might want to provide goggles and those inexpensive paper facemasks to keep paint out of eyes and noses. Don't encourage them to paint each other since it won't come out of clothing and can be hard to remove from skin.

When everyone is finished, have each guy take a turn explaining to the rest of the guys about his "artwork." Some may not be able to explain any significance to what they sprayed at all. That's OK. Try to grab a picture as each one is about to share.

After they've shared, find a place to sit and talk about it—preferably over food.

SHOPPING LIST

- 4x8-foot sheets of thin and cheap plywood, paneling, or sheetrock (about 1 sheet per 2 guys)

- spray paint (variety of colors and at least 1 can per guy)

- plastic sheeting or dropcloth to protect areas from overspray

- digital camera

● TAKE IT TO THE NEXT LEVEL

You want to start the guys thinking about what kind of "mark" they want to make in life. Even at this age it's not too early to start thinking about the difference they might want to make in the world. Some guys may find this difficult—they may never have considered this before.

OK, everyone had a chance to "leave their mark" with the paint. Was it hard to describe or express yourself with a can of spray paint? Tell me more about that.

Some guys do this all the time. What kinds of graffiti have you seen? What do you think of it?

This is easier to do if you live in the city than in the country, but see what they say. They may talk about gang signs, names and murals sprayed on walls or train cars, tagging, and other displays.

Whether it's simply a name, a picture, or marking gang turf, graffiti is one way guys tell the world that they were there. It's a way of showing that they exist and that things are a little different because they were there.

Do you feel that most guys need to know that their existence makes a difference? that their life matters? Why or why not?

How do some guys try to prove to themselves and others that there *is* significance to their life—that their life matters?

This should be interesting. While they share about other guys, they may be opening a window to their own souls at the same time. If you'd like to prompt them with further questions to get them talking more, try a few of these questions:

Do you think this is a motivating factor for some guys in sports?

How about in academic scores?

Is it a factor in relationships—like with friends or girlfriends?

Could this be one reason why some guys are "class clowns" or try to get so much attention and approval from others?

Do guys ever do things just to try to prove to their parents that their life matters? How do they do that?

How can this struggle to prove that their life holds meaning get some guys in trouble?

There could be lots of answers here, so see what they come up with. Couldn't it lead some to compromised standards just to be popular?

Think about the need to prove your life matters. Do you think some guys try so hard to prove something because they aren't sure there's a purpose for their life?

This is a deep thought. You may need to repeat or rephrase it. Give guys time to respond.

If a guy feels his life is random or unimportant, will that affect how he lives? If so, how?

What might be some symptoms of a guy who really doesn't see any purpose specific to his life? How might the guy who doesn't think his life truly matters act?

The extreme answer is that they may be suicidal. Explore a bit more. Guys like this may pull away socially, or they may be aggressive and hurtful. They may live for the moment in reckless abandon because nothing else makes much sense anyway. They may immerse themselves in something bigger, like a cause. They may lose themselves in computer games or whatever.

So here's the question. Is there a purpose for life?

| The term *graffiti* comes from the Greek word *graphein* which means "to write." |

After a few minutes of discussion, read:

 "No, O people, the Lord has told you what is good, and this is what he requires of you: to do what is right, to love mercy, and to walk humbly with your God" (Micah 6:8).

What can you draw from this verse about purpose in life? Do you think this covers it all? Why or why not?

After a few minutes of discussion, read:

 "For we are God's masterpiece. He has created us anew in Christ Jesus, so we can do the good things he planned for us long ago" (Ephesians 2:10).

What can you draw from this verse about purpose in life?

How might this truth affect your need to prove your life matters?

Fully embracing this truth, that God has a plan for each of his followers, *proves* that life matters. By understanding and believing this, we can save ourselves from destructive ways of trying to prove our lives matter.

So how do we find this plan? What am I supposed to do if I don't know what God's plan is?

How does Proverbs 16:9 help answer that question?

 "We can make our plans, but the Lord determines our steps."

So let's put it all together. Combine Micah 6:8 (which tells us to live in obedience to God, to be like him, and to walk with him through life) with Proverbs 16:9 (which tells us that God will direct us) and what do you get?

This is so important. When we live in obedience, strive to grow to be like Christ, and walk with God, he will direct us. Then I will find the specific plans he has for me as referred to in Ephesians 2:10. He'll lead me there. Isn't that fantastic? This should be an "aha" moment for the guys. It's freeing, isn't it?

Sum It Up

Some cities have "graffiti blaster" crews, driving pressure washer trucks, who work full time removing graffiti. Now think about your life for a moment. Can you think of anyone who may actually want to erase any worthwhile mark you make in life? eliminate your significance?

Sometimes "friends" don't like to see others get serious about the important things of life. It makes them have to face the facts about their own life—and that's not a place they like to look at. Also, we have an adversary in the realms of darkness, don't we?

The point I'm trying to make is simply this: God has a plan for your life. Sure, a way to live in general—but also some specific things he's planned for you to accomplish. You can know there will be obstacles; there will be those seen and unseen forces who will try to distract you.

We'd all like to accomplish *big* things for God, but don't discount the importance of the smaller things you do that may be part of his plan. What could some of those things be?

Reaching out to someone who needs a friend. Encouraging others to live by God's guidelines. Strengthening the discouraged or those ready to compromise. Leading others to Jesus. Being an example of a true Christian.

We all want to make our "mark" in life. What kind of mark are you going to leave? What will this tell others about the reality of God in your life? What mark will you make on others?

Review Micah 6:8 again. We live in obedience. We grow to be like him. We walk with him. And according to Proverbs 16:9, he'll lead us.

What do you need to do today? tomorrow? this week?

|▭| E-MAIL REMINDER (2-3 DAYS LATER)

- Remind them that God *does* have a plan, a purpose for their lives. Encourage them to leave their "mark" in life by accomplishing God's plan.
- Print out the three verses you shared—not just the references: Micah 6:8, Proverbs 16:9, and Ephesians 2:10.
- Attach digital pictures.

END CHAPTER ONE

TIP:
Be sure you dispose of the paint cans immediately and properly.

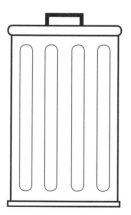

THEME
God can make something good out of our lives,
even though it may not look like it now.

TITLE
Bag Lunch

RISK

LOW   MED   HI

SHOPPING LIST

- eggs (3 per guy)
- sour cream
- butter, salt, pepper
- shredded cheese
- chopped ham, green peppers, onions, mushrooms, bacon, or anything else you might want in an omelet
- sandwich-size plastic bags with sealable seam
- permanent marker
- plates, forks
- pot to boil water
- tongs to lift the bags out of the boiling water
- tablespoon
- access to stove
- digital camera

● PREP

Basically, this is about making an omelet in a plastic bag. You'll definitely need to practice ahead of time. The whole idea is to mix a bunch of ingredients in a bag, boil it, and presto—you have an omelet! The guys will learn how all these seemingly random things come together to make something good. They'll see how certain ingredients they'd never eat individually (like sour cream or butter) can blend with others to make an excellent snack.

Now let's practice. Start water boiling in a pot on the stove. Chop up green peppers, ham, and other omelet add-ins and keep them in separate plastic sandwich bags.

Crack open three eggs and drop the yolks and whites into a new sandwich bag. Squeeze the air out of the bag and seal. Squish the contents around until the whites and yolks are mixed well. Feels like one of those stress-reducing things doesn't it? Open the bag and add 2 tablespoons of sour cream. Repeat the sealing and mixing procedure. Open the bag one more time and add chopped ham, green peppers, or anything else you want. Add about a tablespoon of butter. You might shake in a bit of salt and pepper before squeezing out most of the air and sealing it again.

Drop the bag in the boiling water, and watch the clock. I boiled mine for about 15 minutes before it solidified nicely. Use tongs to handle the bag. *Be careful not to burn yourself.*

If you find the omelet is still a bit runny inside, boil it a few minutes longer or finish it off in the microwave. How does it taste? I was amazed how good it really was.

If you use fewer eggs, boil the bags for less time and finish cooking them in the microwave.

Another prep matter—read the account of Joseph in Genesis. It begins in Genesis 37 and continues through Genesis 48. You're not going to have time to read this whole account with the guys, but it helps if you're familiar with all the events of Joseph's life. Take a few notes on key events that stand out to you to keep them fresh in your mind.

● GETTING STARTED

Keep the eggs and sour cream refrigerated until you're ready to go. You might want to have one or two pots of boiling water started before the guys get there. *Remind them to be careful around the hot stove and boiling water.*

TIP:
This is a great devotion to use on a camping trip.

Give each guy a plastic bag and ask him to write his name on it with the permanent marker. Next, have guys crack the eggs open and put three in each bag. Have them squeeze out the air, seal it, and mix it up good. Repeat for the sour cream. Then let them add the ham, cheese, and other ingredients according to their tastes. Add the butter, salt, and pepper. Finally, be sure they seal the bags really well before slipping them into the boiling water. This would be a good time to grab a picture.

When the omelets are done, have the guys empty their bags onto plates and dig in. This might be another good time for a photo. While they're eating, start your discussion time.

● TAKE IT TO THE NEXT LEVEL

What did you expect this to taste like? Are you surprised at all by how these turned out?

Which of the individual ingredients would you snack on all by themselves? The cheese? ham? green peppers?

What about the other ingredients we used? Which one that we added would you never eat by itself?

If guys don't say much here, prompt them with a few of these questions:

- Would you crack open a few eggs and eat them raw?
- Would you spoon out some sour cream and eat it like ice cream?
- Would you slice a slab of butter and let it melt in your mouth?
- Would you eat a handful of onions like they were candy?
- Would you open your mouth and shake salt or pepper on your tongue?

Some guys might respond "yes" just for the gross-out factor, but it's likely that they'd rarely if ever eat these items unless another guy was daring them.

A lot of these ingredients you'd never choose to snack on. But when you combine them all together and cook the things you like along with those you don't, suddenly we have something that's really good. How is this like life?

Allow them a moment to process this question, and encourage them to answer instead of shrugging this question off. Take whatever they give you and build on it.

What are a few of the good things in life? bad things? wonderful moments? horrible moments?

There are times we're so happy we'd like to shout in complete exhilaration, and other times we'd like to scream in total frustration.

Exciting times. Boring times. Times it seems we can do nothing wrong and other times it seems we can't do anything right.

In your own life, what percent of a typical day is exciting and good versus what percent is boring or not good?

Answers will vary widely depending on tons of factors. You're getting them ready to see the big picture.

Sometimes the bad seems to totally outweigh the good. How many of you ever feel that way?

Ask for a show of hands. Sometimes guys need to see they're not the only one. It's easy to look at someone else and think they don't have the worries, problems, and struggles that you do.

The book of Genesis tells the story of Joseph. Here's a real guy who was on a serious losing streak. His whole life is pretty amazing, but we'll just focus on a few key events from his life.

Review the story starting at Genesis 37. Here are a few of the main events:

Joseph lived a privileged life, but his older brothers hated him. While away from the protection of his dad, the brothers sold him as a slave to a passing caravan. He was taken to Egypt and sold again—all the while knowing nobody was going to rescue him.

Things started going better for Joseph. The Lord helped him by giving him a good attitude and blessing his work, and Joseph's master appreciated him. Then his master's wife wanted to turn him into her sex slave. As a matter of integrity he refused the "invitation"—so she falsely accused him of taking advantage of her, and he was thrown into prison.

Thankfully, the story didn't end there. The ruler, a guy called the Pharaoh, had a troubling dream. Joseph interpreted it, and suddenly Joseph was put in charge of the entire nation of Egypt. The only one with more authority was Pharaoh himself. Joseph got reunited with his very repentant brothers and his happily shocked dad. His brothers were afraid for their lives after what they did to him. But Joseph forgave them for all the hardship they caused him because by now he had an entirely different perspective on it. Listen to how he explained it in Genesis 45:

 Verse 5: "But don't be upset, and don't be angry with yourselves for selling me to this place. It was God who sent me here ahead of you to preserve your lives."

 Verse 8: "So it was God who sent me here, not you! And he is the one who made me an adviser to Pharaoh—the manager of his entire palace and the governor of all Egypt."

And in Genesis 50:19-20 Joseph replied, "Don't be afraid of me. Am I God, that I can punish you? You intended to harm me, but

l The world's largest omelet was made in Madrid from 5,000 eggs by chef Carlos Fernandez. It weighed 1,320lbs. l

God intended it all for good. He brought me to this position so I could save the lives of many people."

"...but God intended it all for *good*."

How do you think Joseph felt in the middle of all those situations of being a slave, being falsely accused, being thrown into prison? Remember, he was a regular guy just like you. What would you have felt if it were you?

Do you think you would have been able to forgive your brothers in the end? Why or why not?

Was there any *possible* way Joseph could have guessed that God was going to do such amazing things with his life?

What if after months in prison Joseph threw his belt over a wooden beam and hanged himself? What would he have missed?

What was it about Joseph that let him see all these bad things working together for good?

Can any of you share about a time where God took bad things and turned them into something really good in your life or someone you know?

Be ready to share a story from your own life as well—you're a great example!

Sum It Up

What if we tried to make that omelet only with the ingredients we liked? What if we didn't add the raw eggs or sour cream or butter? And what if we didn't boil it? What would we have had?

In our omelets we mixed in the good and the bad and got something great. Life can be the same way. The hard stuff might be necessary. God can use it to make something very good—but it might take a long time.

Read Romans 8:28.

 "And we know that God causes everything to work together for the good of those who love God and are called according to his purpose for them."

How does this verse along with the story of Joseph encourage you?

There are a few points you can make to wrap up this devotion. Remember, the guys in your group might be going through incredibly hard situations, so a "pat" answer isn't going to help them. Choose the words that will be the most encouraging.

- Hard times teach us to trust God—to rely on him.

- Hard times can cause us to follow him closer and to turn away from damaging sin and addictions.

- Hard times can help us to combat pride and have humility.
- Hard times can cause us to be more thankful.

Let me encourage you to love God and desire his purposes for your life. Then trust him to work all the things together, the bad and the good, to make something that is very good for us—something you can't possibly foresee.

Be sure to allow time to pray together, especially if guys have shared about some rough situations in their lives.

|⊡| E-MAIL REMINDER (2-3 DAYS LATER)

- Encourage the guys to love God, desire his purpose for their lives, and trust him to work the good and the bad out for their good.
- Let them know you're praying for them.
- Add a one-line teaser about the next session you've planned for them.
- Attach a digital photo.

END CHAPTER TWO

TIP:
Clean-up is easy! Just toss the sandwich bags into the trash.
And eggshells and left-over veggie parts can be added to your compost pile.

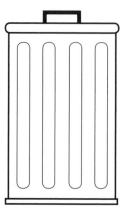

THEME

Guys take potentially destructive risks, often just to look cool in front of others. We'll talk about using that gutsy energy to do constructive things for God.

TITLE

Hot Stuff

● PREP

Testing is a must—but you'll enjoy it. This should *not* be done indoors in a fireplace.

Get a nice fire going in an outdoor fire pit or on an open charcoal grill before experimenting with the powdered coffee creamer. Holding the container about 4 feet above the tips of the flames, shake some powdered coffee creamer over the blaze. When mixed with sufficient air, the coffee creamer will ignite with a flash the moment it hits the fire.

Guys seem to naturally gravitate to a fire, and when you use a flame-boosting agent like this, you'll have no problem getting participation! My son, Luke, and I used up over half the container just messing around with this.

I also noticed Luke took greater and greater risks. He wanted to see how high he could get the flame, and burned his thumb in the process. Nothing serious, but it illustrated my point perfectly. (And…that's just another safety note to you about setting limits so none of your guys get burned.)

After you test this you'll have an idea of just how many containers of powdered coffee creamer to pick up. Buy enough so each of the guys gets to have some fun with it.

Prep yourself for the Bible discussion by reading 1 Samuel 13:16–14:23 ahead of time to become familiar with the events from the life of Jonathan.

RISK

LOW   MED   HI

SHOPPING LIST

- powdered coffee creamer such as Coffee-mate (one or more containers, original flavor)

- outdoor fire pit and supplies (paper, wood, fluid, lighter) to start a fire, or you could do this over an active flame in an open charcoal grill

- safety goggles for each of the guys

- bucket of water or hose nearby to douse the flame when done

- digital camera

GOGGLE ZONE

TIP:

This is a great devotion to use on a camping trip.

● GETTING STARTED

Enlist the guys' help to get a fire blazing in the fire pit. Once the fire is going well on its own, explain that you want to experiment a bit with the reaction powdered coffee creamer has to the flame.

Be sure to cover basic safety procedures! Each of the guys should wear safety goggles—no exceptions. Also, allow only one guy to handle the powdered coffee creamer or be close to the fire at a time. Have a hose turned on or a bucket filled with water nearby.

This will be a good time to get some photos. With a digital camera, it can be hard to time it just right so you capture the flame at its maximum. If you have that problem, see if your camera has a "slow synchro" flash setting. With some cameras it may be listed as a "night scene" option, often symbolized with a crescent moon icon or a person in the foreground with a moon and star in the background. Make the change to the setting, and hold the camera *very steady* or lean it on a fixed object. When you're ready to press the shutter release, have the person with the powdered coffee creamer keep a continuous but light flow of the creamer going for several seconds. The shutter will hang open a bit longer after the flash fires, making it much more likely that you'll catch the full flame effect.

Take note of any "close calls" the guys have where the flame shoots up at them. Usually these will be marked with a burst of laughter from the other guys. You may be able to refer to those times during your discussion. Once every guy has had a turn, get them to sit around the fire to talk about it. Put the creamer away so it's not a distraction.

● TAKE IT TO THE NEXT LEVEL

OK, poking around in a fire is always something we like to do, but what was it about the powdered coffee creamer that made this even more fun?

Did anybody get burned or get a little bit too close and feel the heat? Did that stop you from trying it again? Why or why not?

How about some of you others? When you saw the flame shoot up by someone's face, did you make up your mind you weren't going to try it, or did it make you even more anxious for your turn?

To a certain extent, we like thrills. We like doing something just a little bit daring—a bit risky. Maybe it's for the rush we get doing it. Maybe it's just expressing our quest for freedom. There are other times we take risks even though a part of us is afraid, especially when others are watching. Why do we still take chances at times like that?

Sometimes it may be to get attention or approval from others. Maybe it's to prove something to ourselves or others. Guys take risks to appear confident.

TIP:
Do not do this experiement when conditions are windy.

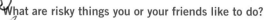

Playing w/ Fire

What are risky things you or your friends like to do?

Be sure you have a story of your own to share about something you did as a younger guy—or that a friend did if you weren't much of a risk taker.

Were the things done generally constructive or destructive? Was there any kind of lasting benefit?

We
Say whether you agree or disagree with this statement: *The risks guys take, especially when they're trying to impress others, have a low level of lasting benefit.* **Explain why you agree or disagree.**

When a guy takes an extraordinary risk, others may somewhat admiringly call him things like "crazy" or "nuts." They may say, "He's a wild man."

Have you ever thought about guys who take risks for God? We usually call them heroes! Let me share a story about a guy named Jonathan from the Bible.

Read 1 Samuel 13:16–14:23 aloud (use your best drama skills—it's an exciting story!). Here are a few points you might want to draw out:

- Israel was at a low point. King Saul's army was reduced to only 600 men.

- The Philistines amassed a huge army and plagued the nation of Israel with raiding parties.

- Philistine raiders captured every blacksmith so the Israelites couldn't make weapons. Eventually, only King Saul and his son Jonathan had real swords.

- Men in Saul's army were so afraid they began defecting. Some actually joined the Philistine army. Others went into hiding.

- Jonathan felt antsy. He wanted to do something. Something risky.

- Believing God could bring them a victory, Jonathan sneaked out of camp with his armorbearer and the two attacked a Philistine outpost.

- As the two boldly walked into the enemy camp, they killed 20 Philistine warriors.

- God used this act of faith by Jonathan and added an earthquake to trigger massive confusion in the Philistine army.

- The terrified Philistines began killing each other. Saul rallied his army and pursued the fleeing Philistines.

- The Israelites who had defected returned to help the king.

- The Israelites won a huge victory against their enemies— and it all started because Jonathan took a risk.

l Nestlé Coffee-Mate, introduced in 1961, was the first powdered non-dairy creamer. l

Now, imagine Jonathan before he left camp with his armorbearer. He's feeling restless. He feels he needs to do something. What if he had used that restless energy in a different way? Instead of attacking the Philistines, what if he had decided to pull pranks on some of the Israelite soldiers hanging around camp? What if he had settled for throwing coffee creamer on the campfire?

The guys might laugh at this, but give them time to imagine a few other things that Jonathan might have chosen to do instead. What can they come up with?

Jonathan could have used that energy to do something that wouldn't have benefited anyone. Instead, he did something that had a lasting benefit—something that pleased God.

What about you? Do you want to take risks that please God, or are you content to do things that might just get a laugh from others?

What are some risky, but God-pleasing, things we can do?

Take your time here. Let them share. Here's a short list to help prime some discussion if you need it. You want them to see there are things *they* can do.

- Take a stand for your faith with friends or in a classroom.
- Bow your head and thank God for your lunch before you eat at school or in a restaurant.
- Talk to your friends about Christ.
- Invite friends to your youth group at church.
- Be honest when you did something wrong, even though it may result in punishment.
- Tell someone you're sorry. Ask for forgiveness.
- When someone is mean to you, be genuinely kind in return.
- Don't just do what your friends are doing if you know it wouldn't please God. Decide to walk with integrity instead of run with the crowd.
- Walk out of a movie or party that wouldn't please God.
- Refuse to give in to pressures to be sexually active on a date.
- Stand up for someone who is being made fun of.
- Reach out to others—especially those who your friends may consider "losers." These people are often lonely and struggle with self-confidence. Walk across the room to talk to someone who isn't in your social circle.
- Pray for someone you can't stand.
- Pray that God will change you into the guy he wants you to be.

TIP:
This is also a great time to talk about men who have courageously taken risks to share the message of Jesus—men who have literally given their lives such as Jim Elliot, Bruce Olson, and Martin Burnham. Perhaps your church supports missionaries who have harrowing stories to tell of what it took for them to share their faith in another land.

Jonathan took a risk. Out of a whole army of men, he alone decided to put his faith in God into action. He was a hero. Isn't that the type of guy you'd like to be?

It doesn't have to be big things. What can you do tonight? tomorrow? this week? Is there something that comes to your mind?

Encourage guys to share what they're thinking of doing—it's a good way to hold each other accountable, and you can follow up on those actions in your next session.

Now ask yourself some other questions. Are the risks I'm taking worth it in the long run—might there be a lasting benefit? Is this something I feel God wants me to do, or that I believe will please him?

Let me share Philippians 4:13 with you.

 "For I can do everything through Christ, who gives me strength."

That's the attitude Jonathan took—and today we know him as a hero. I pray you'll do the same.

TIP:
Be sure to completely douse the fire with water before you leave the area.

|◯| **E-MAIL REMINDER (2-3 DAYS LATER)**

- Recap your time together in just a few lines.
- Challenge them to do something "risky" for God today.
- Print out Philippians 4:13 for them.
- Attach digital photos.

END CHAPTER THREE

Don't waste time wishing you were like someone else. God can do great things through you, no matter how little you think you have to offer.

TITLE
Get More From Less

● PREP

You will need very little prep for this one. The main thing is to select the squirt guns carefully. Basically, be sure one of the guns is so clearly better than the others that every guy wishes he got it.

Next, you'll need to find a place to have this devotion. Ultimately, you're going to have a squirt-gun war, so this probably isn't the kind of thing you'll want to try to pull off indoors. Think about where you want to do this and how you'll define the boundaries of the war zone. For example, you might bring a rope or a garden hose and lay it out in a circle.

Just before you get together with the guys, fill all the squirt guns with water and then label them with numbers (if you decided to have matching numbers on slips of paper in a cup for a drawing) or put them in a duffel bag so you're ready for a random drawing.

You'll also want to read the account of the boy sharing his lunch from John 6.

Optional Method—If you really don't want the guys to get wet, set up a target for them to aim at instead of having them shoot at each other. You'll want to set the target at least 12 or 15 feet away, which will already be out of range for most of the guns. See how inadequate or cheated some of the guys will be feeling? When I did this one, I actually used a paint-ball marker (gun) for the ultimate weapon. It was totally effective. Everybody wanted to try the paint-ball gun, but only the one guy got the chance. It frustrated the others wonderfully.

● GETTING STARTED

Have your drawing so each guy gets a squirt gun. Ask them not to shoot it until you give the word. If you hint that they'll need every bit of ammo they have, you'll probably get more cooperation. You may want to take note of the reactions the guys have when they see the squirt gun they drew as compared with what others got. You may be able to use that during your discussion time later.

Now, assuming you've opted to do the "every-man-for-himself" version of this, go over the ground rules. These should be pretty simple.

- Stay within the "war zone" boundaries.

- Shoot until you're out of water.

- When you run out, sit down **within** the boundaries.

RISK

LOW   MED   HI

SHOPPING LIST

- 1 squirt gun for each of the guys (Important note: Have a variety of sizes from small, wimpy squirt guns to at least 1 powerful super-soaking type.)

- towels to dry off with afterward

- length of rope or garden hose to mark off a boundary

- some kind of system so the guys select their squirt gun randomly (such as drawing slips of paper from a cup)

- safety goggles (a good idea, but not essential)

- digital camera

The thing is, even when they run out of water they can still be a target for the other guys. (Sitting ducks is more like it!)

Now, you may get a little whining from the guys with the wimpy squirt guns. Perfect. On your signal the little water war starts. This is a perfect time to take pictures—but you're going to want to play this game, too. For this session invite someone (perhaps a sister, wife, or girlfriend?) to join you as a photographer—and make that person off limits for the water so the camera isn't damaged. After the last player runs out of water, take a group picture and toss around towels to dry off a bit.

● TAKE IT TO THE NEXT LEVEL

Gather everyone for discussion. (Do you have food to share?)

How did you feel about the squirt gun you got?

How did you feel when you ran out of water and had to sit down while some of the other guys were able to keep shooting?

Did any of you find it frustrating? Did anybody feel it wasn't quite fair? Why or why not?

I imagine a lot of guys felt a bit cheated that they didn't get to choose the gun and that the guns weren't equal in size and capability.

If we were to fill the guns and do this again, how many of you would want to use the smallest gun? the biggest one? Why?

I purposely didn't make all the guns equal, and you didn't have any choice about which squirt gun you got. Some of you had extreme disadvantages while others seemed to get all the breaks. When have you felt like this was the way life is set up for you?

Encourage guys to share about times they felt like others had the upper hand or got all the breaks—and they didn't get any advantage. It would be great if you had a story from your own life to share, too.

What kinds of things do we have no control over—God decides them for us—some of them even at birth?

This might include basic looks and natural abilities. Their basic intelligence. The family they were born into. The brothers and/or sisters they have. Their basic personality, maybe their popularity to some extent. It might include the wealth of their families, the jobs their parents have, the city or area where they live, and other factors that can change but that they don't have any control over.

Raise of hands here. Does anybody here feel that God may have been a little unfair to you? Do you feel like maybe he showed a bit of favoritism to others? Have you ever felt like God cheated you in some way when it comes to these things?

This is a huge moment. Give them a bit of time. Patiently draw it out of them. If they volunteer specifics, that's great. Don't expect them to share how they feel inferior. It's enough if they share that they feel they've been wronged in some way. The guys may be surprised that almost everyone feels that way in some area of their life. Maybe you'll want to share a personal example.

Let me tell you a story about a guy in the Bible who didn't have much, but that didn't stop him from making a big impact.

In your own words, briefly recount the story of the boy who gave his small, insignificant lunch to Jesus in John 6 (or you can read it aloud from the Bible).

TIP:
You can also adapt this devotion and use the story of Gideon in Judges 6.

Five little loaves of bread and two fish. It didn't look like much, but the guy gave it to Jesus. Jesus prayed and started breaking it into pieces to feed the people. He actually multiplied it so the lunch never ran out. In the end, there were 12 baskets of leftovers.

There was no way he could have foreseen all that Jesus planned to do. Think about it. Was there any way the guy with the lunch would have even imagined his lunch could feed 5,000 people? The lunch was designed for one. Jesus multiplied the power of that meal by over 5,000.

If you had been this boy, what do you think you'd have been thinking when Jesus picked up your lunch?

What would you have been thinking after that food fed everyone?

Now I want you to think about yourselves for a minute. It's easy to focus on our inabilities. It's natural to look at others and feel, "If I only had what he has…I'd be doing OK." We feel like we did in the war zone, out of ammo and getting nailed by someone else.

Let's see what the Bible says.

 "And God will generously provide all you need. Then you will always have everything you need and plenty left over to share with others" (2 Corinthians 9:8).

This does sound true when it comes to the boy in the Bible story. Do you believe it's true for you? Why or why not?

Here's another verse to consider:

 "Now all glory to God, who is able, through his mighty power at work within us, to accomplish infinitely more that we might ask or think" (Ephesians 3:20).

How does this verse encourage you, especially when life seems unfair?

What do you think God accomplishes in us or through us when life seems unfair?

When we look at these Scriptures, how might we be like the guy with the loaves and fish?

We want them to bridge the gap here between a story in the Bible and themselves.

Is it possible that God can take the little we have going for us, and all the disadvantages we feel we have, and make something with it all that is amazingly beyond what we could imagine?

If we believe God can do this, what should our attitude be about those situations that are truly out of our control?

What should our attitude be toward others who seem to have better advantages? those we feel jealous of or resentful about?

Don't waste your time wishing you were like someone else. God wants to do a work in us that will be unquestionably credited to him.

Encourage guys to reflect on the areas where they feel totally inadequate. They're probably not going to share those out loud—but they know them in their hearts. How can they give these areas to God and also give God control? Challenge them to at least think on these things even if they're not ready to share about them out loud. And if any do share, be supportive and authentic—don't gloss over what seems a difficult situation to the young man.

The guy in John 6 gave what he had to Jesus. Each of us needs to do the same, trusting God to do things we can't possibly see, predict, or fathom. Put it in your own words, but you'll want to get this truth across to them. There is tremendous hope in this truth—hope that each guy needs to hang on to.

There's no way we can anticipate what God can do through our limited abilities or obvious inabilities. If we give what we have, no matter how insignificant, completely to God, he can multiply it thousands of times more than we imagine. Think about that statement. Do you believe it?

Let me read it again. If we give what we have, no matter how insignificant, completely to God, he can multiply it thousands of times more than we imagine.

It's like connecting your squirt gun to a fire hydrant. Limitless.

Let's not waste our time wishing we were like someone else or resenting others. The real issue is, are you willing to give what you have to God and trust him with the results?

Let each of the guys keep their squirt gun as a reminder of this truth. And if you have time, go ahead and have a few more rounds of water wars!

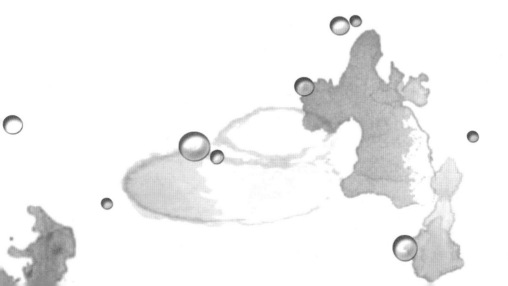

⌷⌷⌷ E-MAIL REMINDER (2-3 DAYS LATER)

- Sum up the main point of the session in two or three lines.
- Include a little teaser line about the next devotion, encouraging them to come next week.
- Attach a digital photo or two from the squirt-gun fight.

END CHAPTER FOUR

> **TIP:**
> Don't sit on the sidelines.
> Get wet!

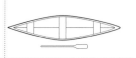

THEME

Compromising the values and principles God has given us to live by will eventually sink us.

TITLE

Boating or Floating?

C | 05

CHAPTER

● PREP

The main prep will be borrowing the canoe or rowboat and finding a good place to launch it. If you don't have a friend or someone at church that has one, check a local park district or camp.

Trying this ahead of time may prove to be difficult unless you have some friends who can give you a hand. If that's the situation, be sure you've at least gone to the location you plan to launch the rowboat or canoe to check it out. Be sure you've looked into matters related to permits or other requirements for boating in your area.

Inspect the canoe or rowboat to be sure it has some sort of built-in flotation so it floats instead of sinking to the bottom after it gets swamped.

Also double-check that the life jackets are United States Coast Guard (USCG) approved and are in good condition (free from rips, and so on).

Don't shortcut safety procedures.

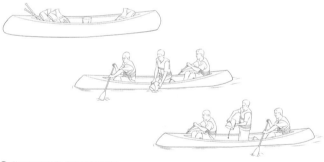

● GETTING STARTED

Once you're at the lake or other body of water, explain that three guys will go out in the canoe or boat at a time. Two will be paddling to a set spot and back, while the third guy uses a bucket to try to swamp the boat before they get back to land. One paddles from the front, one from the rear, and one with the bucket sits in the middle.

If there are guys who are not willing to participate, don't force them. But the fact that there's competition involved with two trying to paddle fast while the other is trying to swamp the boat makes it interesting—and most guys are up for the competition.

A few safety reminders:

1. *Make sure every guy in the boat wears a USCG-approved life jacket that corresponds correctly with his weight. Be sure all straps are securely strapped.*

RISK

LOW   MED   HI

SHOPPING LIST

- canoe or rowboat with paddles or oars
- United States Coast Guard-approved life jackets for each guy in the canoe or rowboat
- bucket
- towels for the guys
- digital camera

TIP:
This is a great activity to try while at camp or on a camping trip. You can also do it in a large pool if you're not near a lake.

TIP:
Don't take on the jobs of timekeeper or photographer while guys are in the boat. You need to stay focused on their safety.

2. *Make sure every guy going in the canoe or boat knows how to swim. Don't assume anything. If a guy doesn't know how to swim, keep him onshore and make him your official photographer or timekeeper. Don't let him in the boat even if he feels secure with a life jacket. He may still panic when it swamps—and that wouldn't be good.*

3. *Always have a cellphone with you to make a call in case of an emergency.*

4. *For safety reasons, it's best to paddle alongshore in shallow water rather than head away from the shore. The guys can touch bottom and reach shore easily after they swamp, it will be easier for you to assist them if there is a problem, and it will allow for better pictures.*

Once you've got a group of three guys ready to go, have someone onshore start timing them and let the race begin! When the boat swamps, the three guys need to pull it to shore, empty the water, and let the next team try it.

Now, if you use a rowboat instead of a canoe, the person bucketing will have a harder time swamping it. In this case you may want a second bucket and have two guys filling the boat while only one rows.

If the canoe rolls when it swamps, immediately make sure everyone is OK. After all the guys who can swim have had a chance in the canoe, pull the canoe onshore, get the guys together, and dive into your discussion.

● TAKE IT TO THE NEXT LEVEL

Congratulate the teams on doing a good job. You may want to review the basic statistics—which paddling team lasted longest before swamping, which bucket-slinging saboteur sank the canoe quickest, and so on. Then move on to some questions.

How far do you think you could have paddled if someone hadn't been bucketing water into the boat?

How much water did you take in before it started to affect your speed or your ability to paddle or steer?

Can anyone describe the changes you felt in how the boat or canoe handled as you took in more and more water?

The canoe was designed to maneuver well in the water, as long as the water wasn't *in* the canoe. That's pretty obvious. Let me put it another way. A canoe is made to float on the water. When water gets in the canoe, you've got trouble.

I want you to imagine that the lake (or river or pond) is the world. By that I mean our culture, our culture's way of thinking. Now imagine the canoe is you as a Christian.

How is the world, our culture, *different* from what God wants it to be?

If the guys aren't coming up with many examples, prompt them with a few of these thoughts:

- *What about people's attitudes?*
- *How do non-Christians determine what is right and wrong?*
- *How is justice corrupted?*
- *Who do they seem to feel they answer to in life?*
- *How do people compromise to get what they want?*
- *What do people think is the key to happiness?*

Now, how is a Christian supposed to be different from the world?

Encourage guys to give specific examples—perhaps related to matters of love, honesty, fear, kindness, integrity, finding happiness, and so on.

How easy is it for the world's thinking, the world's attitudes, to seep into Christians' lives?

Can you give me some examples?

In case they need a jump-start to begin brainstorming, have some examples of people who compromised God's truth and accepted the world's ways in some area—maybe how it happened to you at one point.

If we allow some of the world's attitudes to influence our thinking and perspective, how does that affect how we function in the world, or our potential impact in the world?

This is the issue. Give them a chance to think and share before you move on to the next questions.

Let's face it. If we aren't living the way God designed us to, we aren't going to enjoy all the benefits of a relationship with God in the long run either.

Romans 12: 1-2 says, "And so, dear brothers and sisters, I plead with you to give your bodies to God because of all he has done for you. Let them be a living and holy sacrifice—the kind he will find acceptable. This is truly the way to worship him. Don't copy the behavior and customs of this world, but let God transform you into a new person by changing the way you think. Then you will learn to know God's will for you, which is good and pleasing and perfect."

How would you put this verse into your own words?

What do you think it means for your own life?

TIP:
Additional verses on this topic you might want to use are James 4:4; 1 Peter 2:11; and Colossians 2:6-8.

Sum It Up

Christians are to be in the world, like the canoe was in the water. But the world isn't supposed to be in *them*. If we're letting the attitudes

and values of the world seep into our life, we're in trouble. It's like a canoe half-filled with water—totally unstable.

That's living dangerously. Instead of boating, we'll just end up floating or treading water. Our relationship with Jesus isn't doing much for us. We're "saved," we have a life jacket, but we aren't living at all up to the potential God intended for us.

If a boat is taking on water, what is the first thing you need to do?

Plug the leak fast and bail the water out.

How would you compare that to a Christian who is not just *in* the world but *taking the world into* his attitudes and actions? What action would you recommend?

When do you feel like others (or even your own actions) are "bucketing" the world and its attitudes and perspectives into your life?

What can you do about this?

Where in your life do you need some bailing out?

Where do you need help with that bailing, and who could help you?

Remind guys that we can always ask God for help. God can really clean out the stuff that's sloshing around in our canoes— stuff that doesn't belong there. Just as the verses in Romans said, God can transform us.

Leave some time for prayer, asking God for help in the areas guys shared about.

TIP:
Be sure to return all equipment in excellent condition, and thank those who loaned it to you!

⌐◯⌐ E-MAIL REMINDER (2-3 DAYS LATER)

- Remind guys to think of areas that may be a source of the world's values seeping into their life. How can they plug these leaks? Can they think of one they need to act on today?
- Remind them to ask God to help them "bail" by transforming their thinking.
- Attach digital photos of the canoe fiasco.
- Print out these words below, and ask them to read and think about them:

"Do not love this world nor the things it offers you, for when you love the world, you do not have the love of the Father in you. For the world offers only a craving for physical pleasure, a craving for everything we see, and pride in our achievements and possessions. These are not from the Father, but are from this world. And this world is fading away *(think of a canoe sinking)*, along with everything that people crave. But anyone who does what pleases God will live forever" *(think of going the distance in a canoe instead of tipping)* (1 John 2:15-17).

END CHAPTER FIVE

| The word *canoe* originiated from the word *kenu*—meaning dugout. |

TITLE
Micro-Mess

C | 06

CHAPTER

● PREP

This is one you'll need to practice ahead of time. Resist the urge to wing it.

You're going to blow up an egg in the microwave. Since every microwave is a little different, it's wise to test this before you do it with the guys. Place the whole egg in the center of the microwave, close the door securely, and set the timer at five minutes on the high setting. Generally, within two minutes the egg will explode with a nice *woooomph!*

When you turn off the microwave and open the door, you'll find egg shrapnel everywhere. It may be my imagination, but I feel I get a better explosion if the egg is cold, like just out of the fridge.

As an alternative to plastering egg all over inside your microwave, you might try putting the egg in a gallon-size plastic storage bag. The ones designed for freezer use are pretty rugged. The nice thing about using a plastic bag is that the mess is pretty well contained. Also, *after the bag cools,* you can hold it up for the guys to see. It makes an effective visual.

Important Note: If you use the plastic bag option, *be absolutely certain that you do not seal the bag.* In fact, I always cut a 3-inch wedge off the corner just to make sure the bag doesn't accidentally seal and create a big combustion chamber. I sealed the bag one time and the microwave door burst open from the force of the explosion. The guys loved it, but I wouldn't do it again.

Two more things you need to do to prepare:

1. *Examine your own life. Are there some things you need to take care of—some things that don't belong in your life?*

2. *Pray that the Holy Spirit will break through to the guys with this devotion.*

● GETTING STARTED

Gather the guys around the microwave *and have them put on the safety goggles.* Give them each a pen and paper.

Tell them you'll put an egg in the microwave, and set the timer for five minutes. Every 10 seconds you'll say "Time." That's their cue to peek through the microwave window, *from a safe distance of at least 5 feet away,* and jot down any changes they observe in the egg. If they see no obvious change, they are to simply jot down "NC" on their paper to indicate "no change."

RISK

LOW   MED   HI

SHOPPING LIST

- **CAUTION:** Safety goggles are required for each of the guys.

- access to a microwave oven

- raw eggs (only need one, but have extras—just in case)

- paper and pen for each of the guys

- digital camera

- 1-gallon freezer-quality plastic bag and scissors (optional)

GOGGLE ZONE

Admittedly, it's tricky to get a good view through the window of a microwave, but generally the guys will be able to see the egg well enough.

To make sure the guys don't get too close, set up a row of several chairs about 5 feet away. The guys can stand behind them.

After the egg bursts, open the microwave door so everyone can see clearly. If you chose to use the plastic bag technique, *wait until the bag cools* before taking it out of the microwave. Have one of the guys hold it, and grab a picture. Now it's time to move into your discussion. (Maybe you'll want to serve scrambled eggs or egg sandwiches while having that discussion!)

● TAKE IT TO THE NEXT LEVEL

Start by having each of the guys hold up the paper where they jotted down their observations. You should see a series of "NC" notations.

I noticed that you listed "NC" on your papers nearly every time you observed the egg. Was there really no change going on and suddenly the egg blew up?

The guys will certainly be smart enough to know that the egg was changing on the inside—but those changes weren't observable to their eyes.

OK. So the egg was changing on the *inside* in ways we couldn't see until it exploded. This is an illustration of life that I hope none of you ever forget. This is a picture of what can happen to us if we choose to hide sin in our lives and leave it there.

What kinds of things do guys hide—things they don't want anyone to see, things that don't belong in a Christian's life?

Notice we didn't say, "What kinds of things do *you* hide in your life?" You may not get much input if you say it like that. On the other hand, if you talk about problems that "guys" have, things "guys" hide in their lives, the ones in your group can share without admitting they have the problem.

There will be the obvious things they'll bring up. Drug or alcohol use, for example. Dishonesty of some sort. Someone may bring up pornography or a sexually active relationship.

You may want to bring up other things that can be hidden in a guy's life, but that may not be quite so obvious. Pride, hypocrisy, selfishness, greed, resentment, or bitterness. Every one of these has the potential to be deadly.

Even though we didn't see any change in the egg, it was changing inside. What kinds of changes can happen inside a guy if he continues to hide something in his life that doesn't belong there?

If a guy keeps doing the wrong thing, his heart will harden. Take a look in the Bible at all the rotten things that can happen in our lives because of a hard heart.

| Microwaves are a form of electromagnetic radiation that is very similar to sunlight and radio waves. |

You might want to have guys work in pairs or groups of three to look up these verses—giving each pair or group a different verse to read, talk about, and then report back to everyone about.

- Mark 10:3-5
- Mark 6:50-52
- Exodus chapters 7, 8, and 9

Here are a few more verses you can read (or have the guys read) and discuss what these mean for their own lives.

TIP:
Additional verses you can use include Isaiah 29:15-16 and Proverbs 22:5.

- "My child, pay attention to what I say. Listen carefully to my words. Don't lose sight of them. Let them penetrate deep into your heart, for they bring life to those who find them, and healing to their whole body. Guard your heart above all else, for it determines the course of your life" (Proverbs 4:20-23).
- "God will judge us for everything we do, including every secret thing, whether good or bad" (Ecclesiastes 12:14).
- "You spread out our sins before you—our secret sins—and you see them all" (Psalm 90:8).

The egg looked OK on the outside, even though there were some real changes going on inside. We can get pretty good at hiding wrong attitudes, habits, or whatever in our lives, too.

We can fool parents or friends. They look at us and see no change. We can look in the mirror and see no change. But if we leave these wrong things in our lives, we're changing inside, guaranteed.

If we leave this wrong stuff in our lives, it's just like an egg in a microwave. Two things you can be sure of:

1. The truth is going to come out.
2. When it does, it's going to make a big mess.

Now's a good time to invite guys to share about people they know who've had this happen. Maybe you know of a sports figure with a steroid problem, someone who was covering up a life of stealing from the company, or something like this.

Sum It Up

When that egg was in the microwave, all of you knew it was going to explode, but nobody knew exactly when, right? In the same way, if we're hiding something, we'll never know when it's going to blow up either. We won't know when the whole thing will get exposed. What does that suggest about what we ought to do about it?

Let me read you something scary from the Bible. Proverbs 5:21-23 says, "For the Lord sees clearly what a man does, examining every path he takes. An evil man is held captive by his own sins; they are ropes that catch and hold him. He will die for lack of self-control; he will be lost because of his great foolishness."

What does this say to you?

Guys, secret sins are deadly, no matter what they are. If you have secret sins, you may think you're getting away with it. You're living dangerously with that thinking. I want to encourage those of you who are dealing with this issue to confess and ask God to set you free.

One more look at the Bible. James 1:21-22 says, "So get rid of all the filth and evil in your lives, and humbly accept the word God has planted in your hearts, for it has the power to save your souls. But don't just listen to God's word. You must do what it says. Otherwise, you are only fooling yourselves."

This is personal enough that guys may not want to share their plans for action aloud, but do encourage them to make a plan for getting out of the trap of sin.

This is serious stuff. In all likelihood, one or more of your guys may be struggling with a sin that can change or destroy his life. Maybe you have a personal testimony of how you fell into the trap of a secret sin and how God rescued you. They need to see the urgency of the whole thing and that failure to act is unbelievably dangerous.

Finally, you may want to offer to talk to the guys one-on-one. Make yourself available and encourage them to call you anytime.

TIP:
Hot water works best to clean this out of your microwave. Add a little lemon juice or vinegar to get ride of the egg smell.

▢ E-MAIL REMINDER (2-3 DAYS LATER)

- Encourage guys by printing out a few of the key verses from this devotion for them to reflect on again.
- Remind them to contact you anytime and add your phone number.
- Add a one-line teaser about next week's topic or activity, and encourage them to be there.
- Attach a photo with the guys and the exploded egg.

Reprinted and adapted from "Micro-Mess" in *Bashed Burritos, Green Eggs... and Other Indoor/Outdoor Devotionals You Can Do With Your Kids* by Tim and Cheryl Shoemaker. Copyright © 2004 by Tim Shoemaker. Used by permission of WingSpread Publishers, a division of Zur Ltd., 800-884-4571.

END CHAPTER SIX

Guys will understand the importance of avoiding traps in life while helping and encouraging others to do the same.

TITLE

Watch Your Step

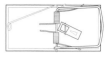

C | O7

CHAPTER

RISK

LOW   MED   HI

● PREP

The cheap, old-fashioned rat traps found at hardware stores will work perfectly. Buy the type with the spring-loaded bar that smacks down when the trap is triggered.

Now, you're going to need to test this nasty-looking snapper out before you do this with the guys. Carefully set the trap, and then use a standard pencil to trip it. The trap should snap the pencil in two. Perfect. Next, test other things to trigger the trap. A carrot? A celery stalk? A pretzel rod? The more variety you have for the small group time, the better.

● GETTING STARTED

Get the guys together and pull the rat traps out. Just the sight of these lethal-looking brutes should get them interested.

Set one trap, and ask for a volunteer to touch the bait pad with a pencil or a pretzel rod to demonstrate the trap's power. When the trap snaps the object in two, you'll probably get a nice reaction from the guys. Now, let each of the guys have a turn. Let them pick the object they want to use to trigger it (pencil, carrot, celery, pretzel rod). So far, so good.

Ask each of the guys to grab a trap and carefully set them up on the floor. Think of this as setting up a minefield to block an easy path across the room. You'll want to space the traps so a person can maneuver around them when someone is leading them.

Now ask the guys to line up and remove their socks and shoes. One at a time, you'll ask them to *carefully* walk through the rat-trap maze. This will be easy for them as they can clearly see the traps. Do note how close they walk to the traps. Do some flirt with the danger? You may be able to use this later.

Now comes the fun part. Ask for a volunteer to go through the maze *blindfolded*. They may need a little extra coaxing. Explain that you're going to lead them around the traps and then anybody who wants to try will get a chance. You can be sure some of them will get just a little uncomfortable. Just to be sure they're getting the picture, remind them what the trap did to the pencil and ask them to imagine what it would do to their toes.

SHOPPING LIST

- rat traps (1 per guy)
- blindfold (bandanna, winter scarf, or even a hoodie worn backward)
- pretzel rods, pencils, celery stalks, carrot sticks, and any other things you can use to test the trap
- safety goggles
- digital camera

TIP:

Extra Caution—*Rat traps can be dangerous!* Keep fingers and other body parts away from these traps. And be aware of flying bits of the broken objects—you may want to have guys wear safety goggles to be sure no slivers of wood or other items land in their eyes.

Now, direct your attention to the barefoot volunteer in front of you. Explain what you're going to do by saying something like this:

After you're blindfolded, I'm going to stand in front of you, put my hand on your shoulders, and guide you through the maze. Are you willing to try?

You can't force him to do this, and you can't blame him if he bails. If he doesn't want to do it, try for another volunteer. When the blindfold is in place, instruct him to hold on to you like you are to him. You'll be standing toe to toe, and he might even want to put his toes up on your shoes just a bit. And yes, *you'd* better wear shoes.

TIP:
Be sure *you* are the one leading the guys through the maze— not one of the guys in the group.

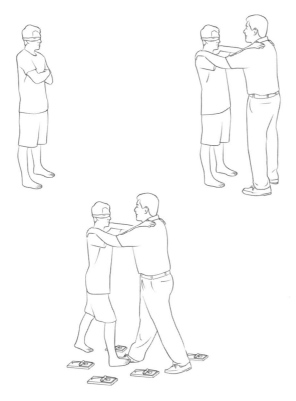

Hand your camera off to one of the other guys, and be sure they take a picture as you inch through the maze. Just before you start, coach the volunteer to listen *only to you.* Assure him by telling him to simply trust you and do exactly as you say while you talk and walk him through.

Walking backward, carefully start through the traps. The other guys will probably be making plenty of noise.

Once you're safely across, offer any of the other guys a chance to pair up with you and try it. Again, I wouldn't pressure anyone to do it who has the good sense to back away from this. If others do want to try it, be sure to get pictures.

IThe first mouse trap was invented by William C. Hooker of Abingdon, Illinois, who received US patent 528671 for his design in 1894. I

Ask the guys to trigger each of the traps so they can pick them up and bring them to the discussion. You might start things off by asking something like this:

Life is full of "traps" that can cause us all kinds of pain. What are common traps guys can get tangled up in?

How can these things be a trap to guys? How do they cause pain or damage?

What about the attitude traps? How can selfishness, greed, pride, jealousy, or being unforgiving be traps that can hurt you?

Would anyone like to share how you or someone you know got tangled up in one of these traps?

Talking about a real situation will be powerful. It would be rare for guys to share a personal example, but you may get them to share about a situation they know about. In the event they don't share, be ready with an example from your own life or from the life of someone you know.

When each of you walked through the maze without the blindfold, it was easy to avoid the traps because you could see them. How can we be looking for traps in real life?

Why is it that sometimes we see how close we can get to traps instead of totally avoiding traps?

If you noticed that the guys walked as close to the traps as possible without setting them off, point that out here. Why do we do that? Are we looking for the thrill? Are we hoping to fall? Are we careless and underestimate the devastating effects the traps can cause?

How can we be blind to traps?

Maybe we're just not paying attention. Maybe being in the wrong place or with certain people causes us to face a temptation trap. Maybe we underestimate the danger of certain traps.

Let me read you a few verses.

 "Dear brothers and sisters, if another believer is overcome by some sin, you who are godly should gently and humbly help that person back onto the right path. And be careful not to fall into the same temptation yourself. Share each other's burdens, and in this way obey the law of Christ. If you think you are too important to help someone, you are only fooling yourself. You are not that important" (Galatians 6:1-3).

According to this, what's our obligation to each other?

In this age of "tolerance" and allowing others to determine their own truth, this may be a good point to cover.

What would you say to help a friend avoid a situation that's wrong and likely to hurt them in the long run? Have you ever had to do this? If so, can you share about it?

Read Romans 14:12-13 aloud, or have one of the guys read it.

 "Yes, each of us will give a personal account to God. So let's stop condemning each other. Decide instead to live in such a way that you will not cause another believer to stumble and fall" (Romans 14:12-13).

How could you put this into practice in your own life? What does it mean in day-to-day life?

This is important. The example we are to others, especially those younger than us, can have a huge effect for good or for bad.

Can you think of a time someone tried to keep you from making a mistake or stepping into a trap? If so, how did you react to him or her?

This is a good chance to remind them that God put parents in this role to a large extent. Do we give parents a hard time about it?

What would you think of me if I deliberately led one of you into a trap?

In real life, we can do that to each other. Have any of you seen or experienced that? If so, what happened?

Give them a chance to think. If they need prompts, help them out a bit. Have they ever seen guys try to convince a friend to do something wrong, dishonest, or simply compromising? Have they ever seen guys encourage a friend to hold a grudge, tell parents off, or whatever? Have they ever reinforced a wrong attitude in a friend? Maybe they justified anger, rudeness, or being mean. Or maybe they've known someone who was making a big mistake but did nothing to try to stop them.

Sum It Up

Here are some Scriptures you may want to share or have the guys read out loud together. There's a lot of content here, so pick and choose what you think will work best with your guys.

- "Whoever abandons the right path will be severely disciplined; whoever hates correction will die" (Proverbs 15:10).

- "Take hold of my instructions; don't let them go. Guard them, for they are the key to life. Don't do as the wicked do, and don't follow the path of evildoers. Don't even think about it; don't go that way. Turn away and keep moving" (Proverbs 4:13-15).

- Additional Scriptures: 1 Timothy 4:12; Hebrews 3:12-13.

How are we going to avoid traps?

Get their input and add to it as you feel necessary. Here's a short list of some ideas they might suggest (or that you might suggest):

- Read the Bible to help me recognize and avoid harmful traps (Psalm 119:9, 33-39, 105).

- Identify the traps that I'm susceptible to. Ask a close friend or two to help me steer clear of them.

- Listen to people who warn me about traps (parents, teachers, friends).

We want to help each other avoid the traps. What are practical ways we can help each other avoid traps?

- Be an example (1 Timothy 4:12).

- Confront friends heading the wrong way (Galatians 6:1-3).

- Encourage friends who are making good choices.

If you think the guys in your group are responsible enough to take home a trap and not set it off around younger children or pets, go ahead and give each guy a trap as a reminder to avoid harmful traps and to watch out for each other.

TIP:
Be sure to sweep or vacuum the area well to get up the tiny bits of stuff that got broken in the traps.

|◻| **E-MAIL REMINDER (2-3 DAYS LATER)**

- Give a one- or two-sentence reminder of the need to watch out for traps and to help each other do the same.
- Encourage them to listen to counsel from parents.
- Encourage them to be a good example to others.
- Possibly add one of the Scripture verses.
- Attach a digital picture.
- Add a one-liner tease to encourage them to come next week.

END CHAPTER SEVEN

THEME
Sticking together as part of a Christian community is important to keeping your faith alive.

TITLE

Easy Target

C | 08

CHAPTER

● PREP

As always, test the activity before you try it live with the guys. It's amazing the little things you'll see that can mess you up that you didn't figure on.

If you're starting a fire in a fireplace or fire pit, you may need newspaper and kindling to help start it. If at all possible, try the campfire/fire pit option. This is the way I did it. There is something about sitting around a campfire that leads guys to really open up.

● GETTING STARTED

When you get together with the guys, let each of them select a squirt gun and fill it with water. Expect the guys to test them out on each other. That just kind of goes with the territory.

Now, place one candle on a stand, and light the wick. Ask for one volunteer to stand a set distance from the lit candle and squirt at it until he puts it out. Have the rest of the guys keep track of the number of squirts it takes, and turn it into a competition between them. After the first guy extinguishes the candle, relight the candle and get the next guy up to the line until each one has had a turn. Depending on the scores, you may want to have the two guys with the best scores have a final round to determine the best shot.

Ask the guys to refill their squirt guns. Meanwhile, get your big fire going in the fire pit or wherever. When the fire is burning full force, one at a time invite each guy to take as many shots at it as he did to extinguish the candle. If it took him 10 shots to snuff out the candle, give him 10 shots to put out the fire. The squirt gun should have little or no effect on the fire. After all the guys have had a turn, the fire should still be burning as nicely as ever.

Ask the guys to top off their squirt guns again. For this round, ask all the guys to line up shoulder to shoulder and let them all work on the fire together. *This would be a great time to catch a digital picture.* Let them shoot until they're out of water. Again, the fire should still be burning reasonably well, even after all that shooting.

Have them fill up one more time if you want to run the activity a little longer. Using a stick or fireplace poker, separate a small piece of log or a stick away from the rest of the fire. Ask the guys to work as a team to try to extinguish it. Depending on the size of the stick, they may or may not be able to completely put it out, but chances are they'll do some noticeable damage. After they note this, put the smoking piece back in the main body of the fire. We'll come back to this later.

RISK

LOW   MED   HI

SHOPPING LIST

- small cheap squirt gun for each guy (for best results, avoid super-soaker type guns)

- candle with stand or holder and matches (you may want to have extra candles on hand)

- digital camera

- access to an outdoor fireplace, fire pit, or charcoal grill and supplies to start it

- buckets of water or hose (ready to use)

  Note: If you don't have access to a fire pit or charcoal grill, you might try picking up a small, 14-ounce propane tank with a nozzle on it like plumbers use when sweating copper pipe. You can pick one up at most hardware stores. The one I picked up was made by BernzOmatic.

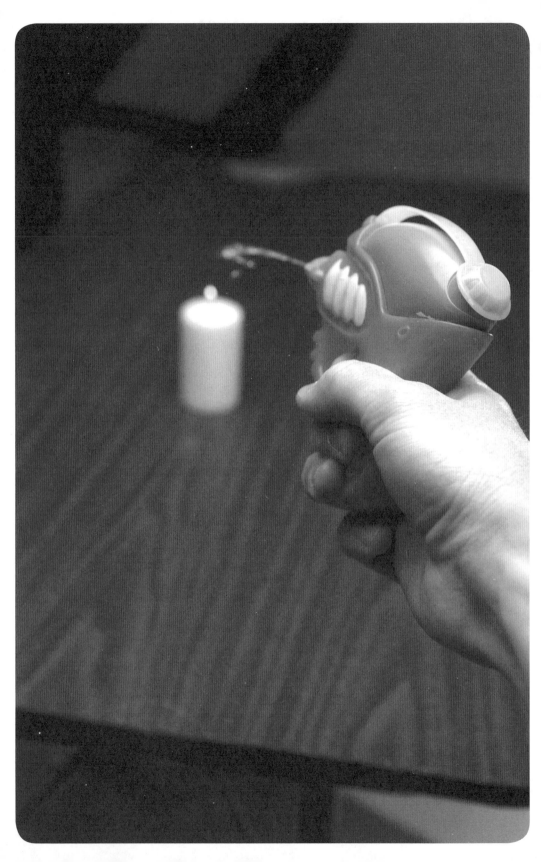

Now you can ask them to sit down while all of you talk a bit about their efforts to extinguish the fire and the candle. One note here. If you have a campfire or fire pit, let the guys gather in close so they can poke at the fire with sticks during the discussion. There's something about fire that attracts guys, and if they can play with the fire in the process, they may actually share a bit more.

● TAKE IT TO THE NEXT LEVEL

If you're doing this by a campfire, you may not get a lot of eye contact as you discuss things with the guys. They'll probably be staring at the fire. That's OK. They'll be listening, and the blaze will only help reinforce your point.

What difference did it make to the intensity of the fire when you alone were unloading your shots into the fire?

The answer should be something like "not much." Perfect.

What about when you all shot at the fire at the same time? What kind of effect did that have?

It may have made more hissing noises and raised some steam or smoke, but most likely when they were done, the fire was still burning strong.

Why is that?

The whole idea is for them to see that the fire collectively was too much to extinguish with a squirt gun. If the water stream hit one log, the piece of wood burning right next to it helped reignite it.

By comparison, how hard or easy was it to extinguish the candle, once you got your aim right?

Obviously, they'll note the candle was much easier to put out than the fire.

All by itself, the candle was an easy target. The bigger fire, made up of a lot of burning wood, stayed strong. This is a picture of the Christian life. What do you think I mean by that?

TIP:
Caution: *You'll be using fire with this one—so keep an extra close eye on the guys.*
This activity must be done outdoors.
And, if it's windy outside, reschedule this devotion for another time. Fire and wind are not a good mix!

TIP:
If the wick of a candle gets too soaked, it may be hard to light again. Have a few extra candles on hand just in case—but only use one at a time.

49

The devil considers every Christian to be a target. He wants to extinguish our effectiveness as a Christian.

How are we sometimes like that lone candle, an easy target?

What kinds of things could the devil use on us to snuff out our effectiveness as followers of Jesus?

Take whatever they give as input and build on it.

Discouragement, disappointments, doubts about our faith or prayer, hard times, falling into some moral failure or sin, loneliness, poor self-image, and fear. These are just some of the ways the forces of darkness can attack us. Check out the story in 1 Kings 19.

Recap the story, or better yet, have the guys turn to it in their Bibles. Elijah slaughtered the 450 prophets of Baal after a spectacular show of God's power. Fearing retribution from the evil king and queen, he fled for his life—and became a target. Elijah took some direct hits of discouragement and fear. His perception of his situation became distorted. This mighty prophet of God was ready to give up in verse 4. He asks God to take his life. After going into hiding, he has the distinct impression he is the only prophet alive (see verses 10 and 14). Left on his own, even a man of God like Elijah became a victim to doubt, fear, and discouragement.

In 1 Kings 19:18 God tells Elijah there are 7,000 others in Israel who haven't bowed to Baal. In other words, Elijah isn't alone. Think back for a second to when you were squirting the big fire and it didn't have much of an extinguishing effect. What are things we can do to protect ourselves from being "extinguished"? How can going to church or hanging out with other Christians protect our faith from being extinguished and protect us, too?

Being around other Christians often has a way of encouraging us, strengthening our faith, keeping our perspective right, and keeping us on track. You're not as easy of a target as you'd be if you were alone. Maybe you or one of the guys has an example to share about trying to stand alone versus standing with the strength of a crowd.

TIP:
You might want to also read or recap 1 Kings 18—it's a pretty awesome story with a huge fire, and it leads right into this account.

Sum It Up

Naturally, there's a lot more you can say on the topic than you can cover during a small group session like this—so don't try. We don't want to overdo it.

We need to be with other Christians for our own benefit, and we need to be there for them, too. Let me share some verses with you.

Choose the verses you think will work best for your guys.

- "Two people are better off than one, for they can help each other succeed. If one person falls, the other can reach out and help. But someone who falls alone is in real trouble" (Ecclesiastes 4:9-10).

- "Let us think of ways to motivate one another to acts of love and good works. And let us not neglect our meeting together, as some people do, but encourage one another, especially now that the day of his return is drawing near" (Hebrews 10:24-25).

- Additional Scriptures: Ecclesiastes 4:12; Proverbs 27:17.

How can you, as a group of guys, be there for each other? How can you be that burning fire that's hard to put out?

Remind them to keep an eye out for each other. Sometimes they need to be ready to encourage or confront each other. They need to help influence the other guys to do the right things.

Now, if you pulled a small chunk of log from the fire earlier and then put it back in the fire a bit later, this would be a good time to bring it to their attention. Show them that even a hunk of wood that is nearly extinguished on its own, once placed back in the fire, will reignite and be a useful part of the fire again.

Maybe one or more of the guys have been a bit sporadic in their attendance lately for one reason or another—or as a group you know of a guy who is "on the edge" with choices he's making. This would be a good time to encourage him to get more involved—or encourage the guys in your group to reach out to him more.

Finally, tell them to keep their squirt gun. Maybe they can put it in their room somewhere. Ask them to remember—every time they see it—that the devil and his forces of darkness want to do everything they can to extinguish each guy's faith.

Remind them that sticking together, like logs in a fire, can help keep their faith burning bright. If they stay away too long, they just may become an easy target.

> **TIP:**
> Is the fire all the way out? Make sure it is before you leave the area!

📧 E-MAIL REMINDER (2-3 DAYS LATER)

- Give them a one- or two-sentence recap on the main point.
- Remind them to encourage their friends in their Christian walk.
- Add a one-line teaser about next week's small group topic or activity.
- Attach a digital picture or two of the activity with the squirt guns.

END CHAPTER EIGHT

THEME
Leading an effective Christian life requires living a "clean" life.

TITLE
Get a Grip

C | 09

CHAPTER

RISK

LOW   MED   HI

● PREP

You'll need to attach the rope to the PVC:

- Mark the center of the PVC length by measuring 6 inches from one end.
- Drill a hole clear through the 3-inch width of the pipe.
- Insert the rope and tie a knot on one end so it won't slip out.

Now, holding the pipe parallel to the ground with a hand on each end of the pipe, you should be able to rotate the pipe so the rope winds up neatly around the center of the pipe.

It's always a good idea to test things before you do it with the guys, so put the Bibles in the bag and tie the bag handles to the long end of the rope dangling free from the PVC. You'll want to try winding it up with the weight in it. To do this, hold the PVC in your hands with an overhand grip. Extend your arms straight out in front of you like a sleepwalker. You should be able to wind this up fairly easily. Now let the rope play out until the bag reaches the floor.

You're going to wind it up again, but this time, slather lots and lots of lotion on your hands first. If you put enough lotion on your hands, you'll have a terrible time trying to wind it up or keep it up. Perfect. Wipe your hands and the ends of the PVC clean and you're ready to go.

If you want to make this a bit more interesting, swap out the lotion for a bottle of baby oil or cooking vegetable oil. Even a tub of lardlike vegetable shortening can increase the grossness factor and may add to the experience.

● GETTING STARTED

When you're together with the guys, pull the PVC contraption out. Attach the bag with the Bibles inside. Tell the guys that you're going to give each of them a chance to hold the PVC and roll the Bibles all the way up. You'll need to demonstrate the right way to do it by keeping your arms parallel to the ground as you wind the Bibles up using an overhand grip.

To make this more interesting, time each of them. One at a time, let each of the guys stand and wind up the load. Mark down their time, and move on to the next guy until all have had a turn. Compare the times and see who was fastest.

SHOPPING LIST

- 1-foot length of 3-inch PVC pipe
- 5-foot length of rope
- drill and bit (only for the setup—guys won't be using this!)
- bottle of lotion
- small plastic or paper bag with handles (or backpack)
- several Bibles to put in the bag
- stopwatch or watch with a second hand
- digital camera
- rags or paper towels for cleaning up
- optional "takeaway"—small bar of soap for each guy

Now tell them you're going to do it one more time for the championship round. This time, you're going to make it a little more difficult. They'll probably suspect you're going to add more weight. Instead, you're going to ask the first guy to hold his hands out in front of him with his palms up. (If you're doing this over a carpeted floor, you may want to put a towel down to catch drips.) Now gob the lotion on both of his hands, from his fingertips to nearly his wrist. Have him lightly rub his hands together for just an instant so the lotion spreads out, and then place the PVC in his hand.

Once again, he'll hold his arms parallel to the ground using an overhand grip. As before, time each of the guys and try to catch a digital photo as they struggle. If they can't seem to get the bag all the way up to the top and it slides to the floor, declare them "disqualified" and move on to the next guy. The guys will probably enjoy teasing their friends until they find out how hard it really is. It's a good idea to have rags or paper towels nearby so the guys won't have to leave to clean up.

After each of the guys has taken a turn, sit them down and make some sense of this.

● TAKE IT TO THE NEXT LEVEL

Start by comparing the times you recorded for each one. First, compare their best time when their hands were clean; then compare their time when their hands weren't clean. You might ask the guys something like this:

On a scale of 1 to 10, 10 being the hardest, how much tougher was it to wind up the bag when your hands weren't clean?

When your hands weren't clean, it was nearly impossible to keep a grip on the PVC. Now let's think about our lives for a few minutes. We can live with "clean hands" or "dirty hands." What do you think I mean by that?

Give them a moment and see what they come up with.

By "dirty hands," I mean allowing sin to be in your life. What kind of sins or things in our lives are we talking about? What kind of sins or wrong things can leave us with "dirty" hands?

You want to be sure each guy sees that the point of this devotion applies to him personally. If you need to prime the well a bit, you might suggest a few things like these:

- What about things like being selfish or jealous or proud?

- What about the attitude that I'm more important than others, or the ways we can be unkind or uncaring when it comes to others?

- Wouldn't these all be examples of dirty hands, of living with sin in our lives?

54

Each of you saw how having stuff on your hands made the task of rolling up the Bibles in a bag nearly impossible. If we have dirty hands because of sin in our lives, how can that make things more difficult for us?

If they need a few prompts, try one or more of these questions:

- How can pride make things more difficult for us?

- How can being selfish complicate our lives?

- How can an attitude of "it's all about me" come back to bite us?

- How can breaking the guidelines God has given us for sexual purity make us struggle in life?

Can anyone share a time where failing to keep your hands clean complicated your life?

This is a great time for you to share an example from your own life.

Now, imagine you're trying to rescue someone. They're hanging over a cliff or dangling off a high bridge. You have this PVC in your hands, and they're on the other end of the rope. There are no emergency rescue workers on the scene. It's up to you to become a human winch. That person's life is in your hands. Winding them up is going to take all you've got, right? OK, here comes a stupid question. What would happen to that person if you had lotion on your hands?

Let the guys respond.

There's going to be a funeral. The same thing can happen in day-to-day life. Anybody have an idea where I'm going with this?

Read the following passage, or have one of the guys read it aloud:

 "Live clean, innocent lives as children of God, shining like bright lights in a world full of crooked and perverse people. Hold firmly to the word of life; then, on the day of Christ's return, I will be proud that I did not run the race in vain and that my work was not useless" (Philippians 2:15b-16).

If I claim to be a follower of Jesus, my attitudes—my whole life— become "exhibit A" as to what being a Christian is all about. But if I have dirty hands, I'm not living in a way that a follower of Jesus should. We've already talked about how these wrong things can have a negative impact on our own lives. But what will be the effect on others? How effective am I going to be when it comes to helping rescue others from eternal death?

I'm not going to be effective at all. In fact, instead of helping them, I may actually hurt them. Can you give me an example of how I might do that?

Resist the urge to beat this to death. Remember, if you can help your guys mine just one nugget of truth right now—something they can take with them—you've accomplished plenty. You shouldn't try to get them to mine all of their gold nuggets in one session.

Sum It Up

After each of you finished your turn with the goop on your hands, you were anxious to get the stuff off. Do you think we should be just as quick to clean up when we get our hands dirty with wrong attitudes or when we do or say wrong things?

Let them digest this for a moment. Don't expect all kinds of input.

Let me read you Hebrews 12:1:

 "Therefore, since we are surrounded by such a huge crowd of witnesses to the life of faith, let us strip off every weight that slows us down, especially the sin that so easily trips us up. And let us run with endurance the race God has set before us."

What are weights that might slow you or other guys down or trip you up?

What would it mean to "strip off" those things?

If we leave sin in our lives, if we don't have clean hands, we hurt ourselves and we're not going to be effective when it comes to helping our friends who need Jesus.

When it comes right down to it, living without clean hands is a dangerous way to go—dangerous for us and for others. Do you agree or disagree? Explain your answer.

We all need to examine our lives regularly. Is there something we need to confess and straighten out with the Lord so we have clean hands?

As a little "takeaway" reminder, you may want to give them each a bar of soap to bring home or throw in their backpack. Tell them to remember the importance of keeping their hands "clean" every time they use the soap.

Additional Scripture: Isaiah 59:1-3.

|◯| E-MAIL REMINDER (2-3 DAYS LATER)

- Give a one- or two-sentence recap of the main point.
- Encourage them to examine their lives, confess as needed, and keep their hands "clean."
- Add a one-line teaser about the topic or activity for the next small group session.
- Attach digital photos of them winding up the bag with Bibles.

END CHAPTER NINE

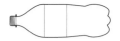

THEME
Guys will see the truth that anger can make a real mess.

TITLE
Fountain of Truth

● PREP

If you try this indoors, you'll probably wish you hadn't. Practice this ahead of time at least twice so you know what to expect. And definitely, outdoors!

On the first practice run have five Mentos ready to drop into the Diet Coke bottle. It's important to get them into the Diet Coke immediately after unscrewing the cap for the first time while the soda has plenty of the carbonated fizz. Drop the five Mentos into the opening and step back. You should get a nice geyser that rises several feet in the air.

Now, let's make the second trial run a bit more interesting. Take the cap from the opened bottle and drill a 1/4-inch hole through the center of it. We'll use this modified cap on a fresh 2-liter bottle of Diet Coke. The smaller hole will force the stream of Diet Coke to shoot higher than it did the first time. The trick is to get the cap on before the chemical reaction takes place. The first time I tried this, the soda fizzed out so quickly, I sprayed it all over myself trying to get the cap in place.

So here's how you're going to beat that. Straighten out the first two bends of a large paper clip. Thread the straight end through the hole in the Diet Coke cap. Skewer five Mentos onto the straight end of the paper clip like a shish kebab. I found it easiest to poke a hole through each Mentos with a skinny finishing nail before sliding it onto the paper clip.

Now, twist off and discard the cap from the unopened Diet Coke. Quickly pull up on the curved part of the paper clip above the modified cap so the Mentos stay tucked high under the cap while you screw it in place. The idea is to keep the Mentos out of the Diet Coke. When the cap is screwed on securely, pull the paper clip free like you're pulling the pin on a grenade so the Mentos drop into the Diet Coke. Isn't that fun?

RISK

LOW   MED   HI

SHOPPING LIST

- plenty of rolls or boxes of Mentos candy mints
- large paper clip
- drill and 1/4-inch bit (You'll only need this for prep time.)
- small finishing nail (to poke a hole in the Mentos)
- supplies to clean up the mess
- digital camera
- 2-liter plastic bottles of Diet Coke (Buy at least one for each of the guys plus a couple to practice with beforehand.)

TIP:
Caution: *Safety glasses are a good idea. Soda in the eyes isn't fun.*

● GETTING STARTED

Pick a spot where it will be easy to clean things up afterward. It would be ideal if you had access to a water hose.

Get the guys together and explain that each of them will have a turn at creating a chemical reaction by dropping Mentos into the Diet Coke. Maybe you'll want to demonstrate it without the modified cap. You can let each guy choose if he wants to try the one with the hole drilled in it or not.

Another variation of this is to set up a competition to see whose Diet Coke squirts the highest or the farthest, whose foams the most or the longest, or whatever.

As each of the guys takes a turn, try to get a picture from a safe distance away. If you've brought extra soda and Mentos, you may want to let the guys try other crazy things after everyone has had their fun. Then pull this together and make the application.

● TAKE IT TO THE NEXT LEVEL

Almost everyone gets in trouble with anger occasionally, but many have *consistent* problems with it. There may even be a guy in your group who witnesses that kind of anger at home or has trouble with it himself. Keep this in mind and pray that God will give you discernment as you talk with the guys.

How is the reaction the Mentos and Diet Coke caused like or unlike an angry outburst?

Can anyone share about a time you saw someone explode in anger?

Can you remember how you felt? Was it scary? funny? stupid?

What about the mess this experiment made—how can anger make a mess of things?

This is really key. We want them to start to realize the destructive power of uncontrolled anger.

In your experience, does an outburst of anger usually accomplish good things or does it make things worse? Can anyone share an example?

We wasted a lot of perfectly good Diet Coke and Mentos on this experiment. How can anger lead to waste?

Are there times you get so angry you want to explode? What types of things light your fuse?

Combining the Diet Coke and Mentos created a chemical reaction. What ingredients often combine to set up an angry outburst?

What elements set the stage for explosive anger? Jealousy? Greed? Selfishness? Embarrassment? What about simply being really hungry or overtired? How does pride fit in? If you really boil it down, pride is probably in the list of ingredients almost every time. Help them see the role pride takes.

Did you notice how most of the things we've just talked about are wrong themselves? Greed, jealousy, selfishness, pride. All of these are sin—and if we don't nip the sin quickly, it can result in anger or rage.

Once the Mentos hit the Diet Coke, there was no way of stopping the reaction. Is it possible to stop anger?

Ultimately, God can help, but if we allow the root sins to stay in place without dealing with them, holding back anger may be like trying to hold back the erupting Diet Coke.

Is anger always bad?

Obviously not. God gets angry. And it's good to be angry at injustice.

What are some bad ways to react to anger, even if we're angry about the right things?

If you need to prompt some thought, what about the person who gets so angry about abortion that they bomb a clinic or hurt a doctor who works in one? Think about people who might be angry for the right reasons but take the wrong path in expressing their anger.

What are some *good* ways to react to anger?

A person can channel anger in a positive way to get motivated to make a difference, like to correct a form of injustice. Getting angry at oneself for blowing it in some way can prompt a person to seek help in conquering the problem or give the person the resolve to do better next time. Anger can drive us to prayer.

How do you usually react when you're angry?

Some people get quiet when they're angry. They stew inside. Is that a problem? Why or why not?

How can reacting in anger hurt you? Can you give an example?

Be ready to share a story of your own about dealing with anger.

There are plenty of places in the Bible that talk about anger. Let's look at some verses.

 "And 'don't sin by letting anger control you.' Don't let the sun go down while you are still angry, for anger gives a foothold to the devil" (Ephesians 4:26-27).

Put this verse in your own words.

What does it mean when it says not to let anger control you or to let the sun go down while you're angry—and how can that give a foothold to the devil?

"Understand this, my dear brothers and sisters: You must all be quick to listen, slow to speak, and slow to get angry. Human anger does not produce the righteousness God desires" (James 1:19-20).

What is this verse saying to you?

Additional Scripture options: Proverbs 15:18; 14:17a; 29:11; 29:22.

Sum It Up

Anger is a huge topic. Pray that you can help them begin to see anger for what it is and that they'll take steps to control their anger.

Is there someone in your life who you tend to get angry with more often than others? Who is it? Why do you find yourself getting angry with him or her?

Often it will be someone close like a parent or sibling. Help them see what is at the root of their anger.

Usually when we get angry it's because something critical to beating anger is missing from our lives. Listen for that ingredient in this passage:

 "Love is patient and kind. Love is not jealous or boastful or proud or rude. It does not demand its own way. It is not irritable, and it keeps no record of being wronged" (1 Corinthians 13:4-5).

According to these verses, when we get angry or easily irritated with someone, what's missing on our part? How do we "fix" that?

Love. When pride, jealousy, or a desire to have our needs met controls us, we are lacking love.

Failure to act in love is wrong. It's sin. If we continue down this path, we're going to make a real mess. We'll hurt ourselves and other people and relationships along the way. How can we change our tendency to get angry and react poorly in that anger?

Maybe you can share a personal testimony. I've often found that when I've felt frustrated with someone, I just couldn't let it go until I stopped and asked God to change me. The Holy Spirit has never failed me. The truth is, God *can* help us. We need to confess and ask for his help.

Asking God to help you curb your anger and love others more is one of the greatest ways you can be an example to others of what being a follower of Christ is all about.

Remember, curbing your anger isn't burying it. We're asking God to get rid of it for good. We're asking him to change us.

Burying anger is sort of like not cleaning up the Diet Coke that sprayed all over. The Coke will get sticky and dirt will start collecting there. It is pretty much the same with our lives. When we bury anger, it seems to attract unwanted problems that are bound to cause us trouble down the road.

Extend the offer to pray with any of the guys who are struggling with anger—whether they express it in unhealthy ways or try to bury it. Remind them that conquering anger is something that may require a lot of attention and going to God often for help. Encourage them to talk to you if they'd like, and remind them that their efforts to change angry words and behavior will be something they won't regret.

▭▯ E-MAIL REMINDER (2-3 DAYS LATER)

- Encourage them to keep asking God for help loving others more.
- Remind them to call you anytime if they'd like to talk more. Add your phone number.
- Include a one-line teaser about next week's small group topic or activity in a way that encourages them to come out.
- Attach a digital photo reminding them of the mess anger can make.

END CHAPTER TEN

TIP:
Hose away any sticky stuff and recycle your plastic bottles. If you did this on a grassy area, see if the area gets greener over the next few days. It did when we tried it!

THEME

White lies, half-truths, and whoppers. When we tell one lie, a whole lot more gush out to follow it.

TITLE

Puking Pumpkin

C | 11

CHAPTER

Note: Don't let the long list keep you from trying this powerful session. The results are well worth it. Don't worry, we'll tell you where to get everything.

RISK

LOW   MED   HI

● PREP

The solution you'll make will create a volume of foam like you've never seen before. When I tested it, I started laughing out loud. I loved it so much I tested it again. Here's exactly where I got my materials:

30 percent hydrogen peroxide

- purchasing source: Check phone directory listing under "Swimming Pool Equipment and Supplies" for local store.

- product description: Baquacil Oxidizer (commonly known as "pool shock")

- cost: approximately $17 for a 1-gallon jug

Note: This is *not* the same as the hydrogen peroxide you'll find at a pharmacy. It's 10 times stronger, so you don't want this to touch your skin. *You'll need chemical-resistant safety gloves and protective eyewear whenever you're handling this solution.*

Important: When buying this or any chemistry supplies, ask for an MSDS (material safety data sheet) and keep it handy. If you end up getting some on your skin or in your eyes, for example, the MSDS sheet will let the person helping know what they are dealing with so they know better how to treat it.

Potassium iodide (KI)

- purchasing source: www.sciencelab.com

- product description: potassium iodide, granular, USP, 125 g

- cost: about $42 (This bottle contains enough to do the experiment 12 times.)

Graduates, beakers, gram scale

- purchasing source: American Science & Surplus, 5316 N. Milwaukee Ave., Chicago, IL, www.sciplus.com

Note: If you know a teacher, you may be able to supply him or her with little plastic film canisters and the potassium iodide to measure it out on a gram scale in his or her school's science department. Ask the teacher to put 10 g in each container, and you'll be all set. Be sure to label each of the containers.

SHOPPING LIST

- chemical-resistant rubber gloves for handling chemistry supplies
- safety goggles for each of the guys
- 2 large pumpkins along with tools to carve and clean them out
- 400 to 600-milliliter (mL) glass beaker (or similar-sized glass bowl)
- large graduate (to measure out 200 mL)
- small graduate (to measure 10 and 15 mL) or teaspoon and tablespoon
- 30 percent hydrogen peroxide
- potassium iodide (KI)—you'll need 10 grams (g) each time you do this
- food coloring
- liquid dish soap
- gram scale
- 5-gallon bucket to set pumpkin on
- plastic to put under bucket and pumpkin
- bucket of water to keep handy while doing the demo
- tea light candle and lighter

I'd highly recommend buying graduates for easy, accurate measuring. Here are some metric conversions if you'd rather use teaspoons or other measuring tools:

- 1 teaspoon = 5 mL
- 1 tablespoon = 15 mL
- 1 fluid ounce = 30 mL
- 8 fluid ounces = 1 cup

TIP:
If you're doing this during a time of year when pumpkins are not available, you could hollow out a large watermelon or other similar kind of fruit or vegetable. You could also do this by carving a face out of a large bucket and putting a lightweight lid over the top so the foam will be forced out of the mouth.

Here we go. Put on your gloves and safety goggles. Be sure to test this one outdoors—preferably on a driveway or parking lot so you don't get the foam on your lawn. You're going to love this—and so will the guys!

- Carve the pumpkins. You'll need a nice big mouth. Set one aside to use later in your discussion.

- Place plastic under an upside-down 5-gallon bucket in a clear area, and set the pumpkin on the bucket.

- Drip food coloring in the glass beaker. Add 200 mL of 30 percent hydrogen peroxide. Add 10 mL of liquid dish soap. Place the beaker inside the pumpkin.

- *In a separate container,* make a solution of 10 g of KI (potassium iodide) in 15 mL of water. Mix until dissolved. **Note:** If you're unable to access a gram scale, 10 g is approximately one slightly rounded teaspoon.

- Pour the potassium iodide solution into the beaker in the pumpkin, *quickly put the lid on the pumpkin, and stand back!*

Note: *The chemical reaction will cause some real heat. Let the beaker cool down before attempting to handle it. I doused the entire area with water after the beaker cooled.*

● GETTING STARTED

Be sure all the guys wear proper safety gloves and protective goggles. No exceptions! Keep a close eye on things because of the strong chemistry.

Run through the procedure exactly like you did when you practiced this. Be sure to get pictures of the guys and the foaming pumpkin.

If you are going to leave the area to talk about it, be sure to clean up the mess first, right after the beaker cools down. Don't leave any chemistry supplies uncapped or unattended.

● TAKE IT TO THE NEXT LEVEL

Pull out the second pumpkin that you set aside. Light the candle in the second pumpkin and set it nearby.

Just a tiny bit of potassium iodide added to the beaker in the pumpkin created all that foam. Was anybody just a little surprised at how the foam kept gushing out so long?

This reminds me of what happens when we tell a lie. It seems when we tell one lie, often more gush out to follow it. Why is that? What other similarities can you think of between the gushing stuff coming out of the pumpkin and lies?

Would anyone like to share a time where one lie turned into a bunch of lies?

They may not be able to think of one or just aren't warmed up enough to share yet. Do you have a story you can share?

What's it feel like to get caught in a lie?

When it's all over, do you ever feel you would've been better off if you'd told the truth in the first place? Why or why not?

Why is lying so bad?

This is important. Lying is all about trust—and trust is foundational. If you can't trust the other person, it affects every area of life with them.

Imagine you have a friend who lies to other people. You know he lies to his parents, to teachers, and maybe to other kids—but never to you. Then one day he tells you something and you *know* it's a lie. What does that do to your friendship?

What if your friend insisted that they were just little white lies? Or that he or she was just telling some harmless fibs? Or that part of it was true, but he or she just didn't give you the whole story. Would that make you feel any better?

I Hydrogen peroxide was discovered (1818) by L. J. Thenard. Hydrogen peroxide, chemical compound, H_2O_2. I

If there is genuine remorse, it's easier to restore trust. When the person who lies acts like it's no big deal or like you're overreacting, it actually raises more red flags, doesn't it?

Does lying hurt the liar? Why or why not?

Take your time here. This is really important for them to see.

Often the reason for lying is to avoid some kind of painful consequence. But how can lying actually make things worse?

Have you ever seen parents punish more for a lie than the thing that was done wrong in the first place? Why is that?

Often the original thing done wrong was a mistake, poor judgment, or outright disobedience. Lying goes a step beyond. Lying is deliberately trying to mislead or deceive.

If you knew you were going to get caught in a lie, would you bother telling the lie at all? Why or why not?

What percentage of the time would you guess a liar gets caught?

What percentage of the time does a liar get caught by God?

Since we know God will catch us 100 percent of the time, lying is pointless unless we feel God is going to let us get away with it. Let's look at some verses that show how God feels about lying.

Have one of the guys read these aloud:

- "A false witness will not go unpunished, nor will a liar escape" (Proverbs 19:5).

- "You will destroy those who tell lies. The Lord detests murderers and deceivers" (Psalm 5:6).

- "There are six things the Lord hates—no, seven things he detests: haughty eyes, a lying tongue, hands that kill the innocent…" (Proverbs 6:16-17).

Notice that pride and lying are listed before murder. Why do you think God hates lying so much?

Deception is at the very heart of lies, and pride lurks right along with it. These are tools God's archenemy, the devil, has forged (see John 8:44).

Additional Scriptures: Revelation 21:8; Ephesians 4:25.

Sum It Up

 "The heart of the godly thinks carefully before speaking; the mouth of the wicked overflows with evil words" (Proverbs 15:28).

The word *overflows* reminds me of the pumpkin. One lie generally isn't enough. We have to keep covering it up with more and more lies. Some people keep lies going for many, many years or even a lifetime.

How can lying become a prison for a person?

The truth is *lies cost us.* They hurt us. Little white lies and whoppers. We make our situation worse when we choose dishonesty.

Let's do three things:

1. Tell God you're sorry for the lies and ask for forgiveness.

2. Resolve to tell the truth. All of it. Always. Ask for God's help.

3. Straighten out things from your past that you need to confess.

Let guys know some of this might be really hard. But the benefits will far outweigh the difficulty.

Have your group think of as many benefits to telling the truth as they can. Here are a few you might mention:

- You'll be in a right standing before God—and that will free you from guilt. It will also give you peace and joy and will allow God to bless you in ways he can't when you're living a lie.

TIP:
Hose down the area to wash away any remaining gunk, and be sure to dispose of the pumpkin appropriately.

- You'll develop a character quality that is priceless and will benefit you for your entire life.

- You'll enjoy more respect and trust from parents and others, which will result in more freedom and better relationships. Do you want that?

The puking pumpkin made a real mess, didn't it?

Lying makes a mess, too, only a whole lot worse. Instead, let's be honest, be like a light of truth (point to the pumpkin with the candle in it), and be a good example for others while we're at it.

Read Colossians 3:9-10 in closing.

 "Don't lie to each other, for you have stripped off your old sinful nature and all its wicked deeds. Put on your new nature, and be renewed as you learn to know your Creator and become like him."

▢ E-MAIL REMINDER (2-3 DAYS LATER)

- Type out Proverbs 24:26: "An honest answer is like a kiss of friendship."
- Add a one-line teaser about next week's session.
- Attach a picture of the puking pumpkin.

END CHAPTER ELEVEN

THEME
We have an absolute need to forgive others of the wrongs they do to us.

TITLE

Sack of Potatoes

C | 12
CHAPTER

● PREP

You won't need to practice an activity ahead of time, but you'll need a little prep work.

For maximum effectiveness, pick up plenty of monster-sized potatoes—the biggest you can find.

Also, be thinking in advance about this whole forgiveness issue. Can you come up with some great examples of forgiveness (or failing to forgive) from your own personal experiences? Did someone forgive you in a surprising or meaningful way?

Most important, examine your heart. Are you holding a grudge against someone? a seed of resentment? Unless you fully take care of the forgiving you need to do, your session with the guys may lack the horsepower it would have otherwise. Ask God to speak to you as you review this session.

Finally, start looking for a potato that has been around in somebody's pantry for a long time. You know the type I'm talking about—a potato that gets those weird, sickly white roots randomly growing out of it from all sides. Ask around, and if you find one, hang on to it for the sequel to this devotion, "Sack of Potatoes 2."

● GETTING STARTED

Let's face it—the need to forgive others can be a real blind spot with a lot of us guys. Take a moment to pray. You'll need the Holy Spirit working overtime to open their eyes.

Get the guys together around the bag of giant potatoes. Ask each of them to grab a potato and a permanent marker. This may be a good time for a picture—before they've begun writing on the potatoes.

Ask the guys to think about a person they have a hard time forgiving. Tell them to write that name across a potato with the marker. Then they'll put that potato to the side and grab a new potato from the pile. Ask them to repeat this every time they come up with another person they are holding some kind of resentment toward. Explain that they can only put one name on a potato.

Here are a few ideas to prime the pump a bit—and you may want to add ideas of your own. As you read them, pause between each one to give guys time to think. Remind them to write the name down if one comes to mind.

- Can you think of someone who embarrassed you or wronged you and you still resent them for it?

RISK

LOW   MED   HI

SHOPPING LIST

- large potatoes—at least 3 or more for each guy
- permanent markers—1 for each guy
- digital camera

TIP:
This works best if you follow up with "Sack of Potatoes 2" the following week, as it focuses on the consequences of failing to forgive.

TIP:
If you're concerned that writing a person's name on the potato might be too revealing—that it might start gossip or embarrass someone— tell guys they can use a nickname or a symbol that represents the person they have in mind.

- Can you think of someone who said some things about you behind your back and you haven't forgiven them for it?

- Can you think of someone who used to be your friend but who isn't anymore and there's still a hurt there?

- Imagine you found a magic lamp. You rub it and the "revenge genie" appears in order to get even with three people of your choice. Who would you ask him to pay back?

If guys are grabbing potatoes and writing names on them, that's good. If not, either you have an unusually wonderful group of guys or you need to pray God will open their eyes.

This might be a good time to interject a personal story. Tell of a time you were wronged and maybe how you struggled to forgive that person or group. Maybe you know a story of a friend who had a hard time forgiving—and maybe for really good reasons. Share it with the guys.

We need to prompt the guys' thinking a bit more. Now, we're not trying to get them to dredge up old resentments that have long been forgotten. We simply want to expose some things that maybe they've tried to bury in a shallow grave. The whole idea is that we want to free them of these things and encourage them to learn to forgive. Let's play this out a bit longer to make sure the guys identify the persons they haven't forgiven.

- How about a girlfriend who broke up with you?

- What about a teacher who gave you a grade you didn't deserve?

- Do you have an unresolved issue with a brother or sister?

- What about your parents? Has one of them let you down in some way, and you just can't seem to forgive him or her?

This could be a sensitive one if physical or emotional abuse has taken place. Or maybe there is a divorce situation that has left one of the guys angry and unforgiving.

- What about God? Are you a bit resentful toward him because of the circumstances of your life in some way?

OK, if the guys are holding any grudges or resentment toward people, hopefully they've written those names across the potatoes. Let's move on.

● TAKE IT TO THE NEXT LEVEL

When we're wronged, we have a choice. Will we forgive the person or hold on to a grudge, resent the person, or maybe even find a way to even the score?

Let's take a look at what God says about forgiveness:

"If you forgive those who sin against you, your heavenly Father will forgive you. But if you refuse to forgive others, your Father will not forgive your sins" (Matthew 6:14-15).

If we don't forgive others, God won't forgive us. Is that fair? Why or why not?

Let's get this right out in the open. I've been truly wronged, yet God will hold off on forgiving me for my petty little sins just because I won't forgive the person who hurt me? Does that sound right?

If they don't come up with it themselves, remind them that God forgives us, *even though we don't deserve it.* To do less than that for others suggests we're ungrateful and proud.

Read this verse, or have one of the guys read it aloud:

"Then Peter came to him and asked, 'Lord, how often should I forgive someone who sins against me? Seven times?' 'No, not seven times,' Jesus replied, 'but seventy times seven!' " (Matthew 18:21-22)

Why would Jesus want us to forgive like that?

For one, that's the way Jesus forgives us. Also, it's for our own good. If we don't forgive someone, it affects *us.* It's like venom that will poison and change us if we don't get rid of it. *At the very root of an unforgiving spirit is pride,* which is not exactly one of the fruits of the Spirit.

Now, does this mean if someone is being abused they need to keep taking the abuse?

This is an important issue to clear up. The answer is "no." We can't cover up for the abuser. We have to expose them, but we also have to forgive.

Let's look at a bit more Scripture:

"Make allowance for each other's faults, and forgive anyone who offends you. Remember, the Lord forgave you, so you must forgive others" (Colossians 3:13).

How would you say this in your own words?

Here's a possible translation:

"Cut people a little slack. We all have faults. When you get offended, don't hold it against them. Get over it. The Lord forgave you when you didn't deserve it. You need to show a little gratitude. Remember, he expects you to offer that same gift to others—whether or not you feel they deserve it."

What really stands out to you in this verse?

Forgiving others can be pretty tough. We understand that God has forgiven us and that we need to forgive others, but honestly, doesn't it sometimes seem like God is expecting you to forgive more in regard to others than he had to forgive with you?

We may tend to think that we aren't so bad and forgiving us was easy on God's part. You may want to remind them that it cost Jesus' life to forgive us. He isn't requiring us to make that kind of sacrifice for others, but we do need to forgive them.

Sum It Up

OK, we understand we're to forgive. But how do we do it? The verse we read in Colossians 3:13 seemed to indicate that remembering how God forgave me is a part of it—that is, having true gratitude for what he did for me.

But is that it? Is there more? Let me read you one more verse:

 "Most important of all, continue to show deep love for each other, for love covers a multitude of sins" (1 Peter 4:8).

Why is love so important? How does it "cover a multitude of sins"?

Love. It makes sense, doesn't it? It was God's great love that initiated the sacrifice to bring us forgiveness. If we love others more, forgiving will come more easily.

Where are we going to find that kind of love when it isn't in us?

True love is a fruit of the Spirit. We need to go to the source of love if we're going to have enough to forgive others. Ask God to give you the love you need.

Gratitude for what God did for us plus love for others—that's the formula that results in forgiveness. We need to ask God to help us with this.

Now here is what I want to challenge you to do:

- I want you to take these potatoes home—every one that you put a name on.

- Every day for the next week I'd like you to load them in your backpack and carry them to school. Carry them every place you'd take your backpack. Next week, bring them all back. OK?

- And one more thing. Ask God to help you forgive these people. Ask him to help you see how much he sacrificed when he offered you forgiveness. Ask him to fill you with love for each of these people—his kind of love.

Nice job. Forgiving others is so important and will make their lives better if they discipline themselves to do it. And it will benefit them not just now, but in the future as well.

- Briefly recap the need to forgive others and how they need to go about it (the whole gratitude and love equation).
- Write out Colossians 3:13 and encourage them to really forgive the people written on the potatoes.
- Remind them to carry the potatoes in their backpacks to school and to bring the potatoes back next week.
- Attach a digital picture of the guys with their potatoes that have not been written on yet.

END CHAPTER TWELVE

TIP:
If you're keeping a potato too, you might want to keep it in an open-air area. Older potatoes can get stinky!

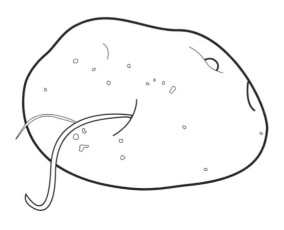

THEME

Refusing to forgive others results in an impaired relationship with God. We end up putting ourselves in a position where we don't receive his blessings, and harm our own well-being.

C | 13

CHAPTER

TITLE

Sack of Potatoes 2

RISK

LOW   MED   HI

SHOPPING LIST

- at least one *old* potato—one that's beginning to decay or that has roots growing out of it. Ask around at work or church. Chances are someone has one like this buried in a pantry.
- digital camera

● PREP

Locating the old potato is the main thing you'll do for prep. Also, think about having this session in a fast-food restaurant where you can order fries and soft drinks for the guys. The fries will provide a nice illustration of how you can make good things from the potatoes, just like forgiving others is so much better than holding on to old resentments.

Also think and pray about at least one story you might share of someone who stubbornly refused to forgive. What was the impact of it on that person's life? This is important, so if you can't come up with an example, ask around. People will generally have a story they can share with you. Your pastor may even be a good source for this. Still stuck? Think about a movie you've seen where someone's failure to forgive led to negative consequences.

● GETTING STARTED

If you opted to meet at a fast-food restaurant, be sure you buy fries for the guys. After everyone is sitting at the table, ask them to take the potatoes from last week out of their backpacks and pile them in front of them.

Take a digital picture of the group of guys at the table. Be sure you can see the orders of fries. Now, ask them a few questions.

How did you like carrying these potatoes around with you all week?

Did they get heavy?

Did they get in your way?

Did anybody make comments about your load? If so, what did they say?

Does anybody have a story to tell about something that happened when you were hauling these around?

How many of you would like to carry these around with you for another day? a week? a month? a year?

If you were able to get your hands on an old potato (or potatoes), this is the time to pull it out.

Here's an old potato that stayed in the pantry a bit too long. Weird looking, right?

What do you think the potatoes you carried around all week will look like in a month or even a year?

How do you think they'll smell?

Last week we talked about the need to forgive others. The Bible made it pretty clear that we're to do that. In fact, we read in Colossians 3:13 that we must forgive others.

 "Make allowance for each other's faults, and forgive anyone who offends you. Remember, the Lord forgave you, so you must forgive others."

Does anything about this verse sound like forgiveness is optional? Explain.

Let's be honest. We don't always do what we're supposed to do, and forgiving others can be one of those things we slip up on. Let's look at what happens when we choose not to forgive.

These potatoes you're carrying got heavy after a while. How can failing to forgive someone—holding resentment against them— actually _weigh you down_ or _slow you down_?

Let them share, but be ready to add to it if they aren't thinking deeply enough yet. The idea that there are tremendous negative consequences for failing to forgive may be a new concept to them.

When I choose not to forgive, I choose to hold a grudge—a resentment against someone. I remind myself how I've been wronged. This is a weight. It saps my energy to keep looking at the negative side of my life. It can lead to real discouragement and emotional problems.

We saw how old potatoes can get really weird looking. In what kinds of ways can a person get "weird" when they fail to forgive others?

Have you ever seen people get consumed by how someone wronged them? They rattle on and on about the other person to the point that you feel uncomfortable. Sometimes they get paranoid or overly sensitive. They read into everything that other person says or does. They get a bit warped.

Sometimes in a family situation, some members of the family won't talk to other members of the family. Or they won't go to a holiday function if they know that other person will be attending. This may be commonplace—but it's so far from God's guidelines that it's plain weird.

Can anyone share an example of this? Do you know a person who won't forgive and acts in a strange way like he or she is obsessed by the whole thing?

If you have a story yourself, you could share it here.

If you keep the potatoes in your backpack long enough, they're going to rot. They're going to stink so bad that everyone around

you will want to get away from you. Not only that, but the sticky, stinky potato juice will get on your backpack or on your books and papers.

How is that like or unlike what happens if we insist on not forgiving others?

Ever notice how an unforgiving person gets bitter? Are they fun to be around? Why or why not?

Have you ever avoided someone because they always seem to want to gripe about problems with the same old person?

Can anyone share an example?

This is a great time to relay the story you have about someone who failed to forgive and the nasty effect it had on his or her own life. This happens so much in families. A real-life story is the best, but don't rule out an example from a movie.

Read, or have one of the guys read, Ephesians 4:30-32:

 "And do not bring sorrow to God's Holy Spirit by the way you live. Remember, he has identified you as his own, guaranteeing that you will be saved on the day of redemption. Get rid of all bitterness, rage, anger, harsh words, and slander, as well as all types of evil behavior. Instead, be kind to each other, tenderhearted, forgiving one another, just as God through Christ has forgiven you."

What reasons are there for forgiving others? What do you think it means to bring sorrow to the Holy Spirit?

This is a good time to remind guys that they are sons of the King and that he has totally forgiven us and saved us. We need to show a little gratitude.

You may want to share the story of the unforgiving servant in Matthew 18:21-35. By failing to forgive, this poor fool lost the gift he had been so generously given and ended up getting a prison sentence and torture as punishment. You may want to quickly recap the story, but read verse 35 word for word:

 "That's what my heavenly Father will do to you if you refuse to forgive your brothers and sisters from your heart."

Sum It Up

Forgiving others is serious stuff. It's essential for:

- having a right, obedient relationship with God.

- being in a position to enjoy God's blessing and avoid his punishment.

- maintaining our own emotional balance and well-being.

Are you ready to forgive those people whose names you wrote on the potatoes you carried all week?

If you're not, put the potatoes back in your backpack. I challenge you to keep them there until you're ready to do it—whether it takes another week or another month.

Take note of any of the guys who choose not to forgive. Pray for them and follow up one-on-one this coming week.

If you're ready to forgive, take the potato for each person you're forgiving and throw it out. You may need to ask God for a little additional love at this moment. Take a moment to pray about each person, expressing your forgiveness—and then toss the potatoes in the garbage and sit back down. Let's take a minute to do that now.

Give them the time to think—to really do this. Since you're at a fast-food place, garbage cans should be readily accessible.

Depending on the situation, remind them that they may need to verbalize this to someone they've been at odds with. "Hey, I realized I'd been holding on to a grudge because of this situation. That was really wrong of me. I've taken care of it with God, and I wanted you to know I'd like a fresh start with you."

Nothing good comes from hanging on to old potatoes, guys. On the other hand, what are some good things that can come from fresh potatoes?

Hopefully, someone will mention the french fries you bought.

When we forgive others, good things come as a result. Like a right relationship with God. Let me encourage you to forgive others quickly and completely from now on. You'll be so much better off for it.

One more thing. How crazy would it be for one of us to sneak back here late tonight, rummage through the dumpster, and find his potatoes so he can put them back in his backpack?

Some of you will be tempted to do that with the people you forgave. You'll get a fresh surge of how you were wronged or whatever, and you'll be tempted to hold a grudge again. Can you see that happening?

I want to encourage you to leave the potatoes in the garbage, along with resentments for others, because that's where they belong.

- Congratulate guys who made the choice to forgive.
- Remind them not to dredge this offense up again, holding it against the offender.
- Attach a picture of them at the table with the potatoes, and maybe include a close-up of the strange-looking one with all the sickly white roots growing out of it.
- Give them a short teaser about next week's topic, encouraging them to attend.

END CHAPTER THIRTEEN

TIP:
Old and rotten potatoes really do stink. Be sure to toss them right away or compost them!

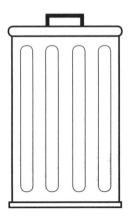

THEME

Christians have a responsibility to be a good example to others, especially those who are younger.

TITLE

Flamethrower

C | 14

CHAPTER

● PREP

As always, you need to test this ahead of time. It will make your time with the guys smoother, and they'll know you're prepared. Either one of those reasons should be enough, but I'll give you one more: It's *so* much fun! My youngest son, Luke, and I experimented with this outside at night and burned through a half quart of rubbing alcohol in no time. We hated to stop.

Pick up a new spray bottle rather than reusing an empty bottle from some other spray product. Two reasons for that:

1. It isn't safe to have a liquid in the bottle that's different than what the label indicates.

2. You want to make sure the nozzle can adjust to spray a *fine mist.* Many spray products have a nozzle that simply pumps a steady stream. That won't work for our purposes.

Now, let's put a flamethrower together.

1. Untwist a wire hanger and straighten it out. Coil one end around the middle of the spray bottle a couple of times, and secure it with duct tape.

2. Wrap the wire around the candle so that it is about 8 inches away from the spray bottle. You'll need to use duct tape to help hold it in place. You may want to cut the candle down to about 6 inches tall so it's a little lighter and the wire arm can support it.

RISK

LOW   MED   HI

SHOPPING LIST

• new spray bottle (with adjustable nozzle so you can spray a fine mist)

• large bottle of rubbing alcohol (isopropyl alcohol 70 percent)

• thin wire hanger

• duct tape

• 2 standard taper candles (they only need to be 6 inches tall or so)

• matches or lighter stick

• safety goggles for every guy

• buckets of water or a hose ready to use

• digital camera

TIP:

Caution! This activity uses fire. Use extra supervision and protection!

3. Twist any excess wire around the wire arm that extends from the bottle to the candle to reinforce it. Also, if you need to adjust the distance, you'll want this excess wire available.

4. Bend the wire arm so the wick of the candle is just an inch or two (horizontally) below the level of the nozzle (but the candle is still 8 inches away).

5. Pour a couple of inches of rubbing alcohol into the spray bottle, and screw the nozzle back on.

Note: *If you aren't outside yet, go there now. Also, wear safety goggles and have a bucket filled with water or a running hose within reach.*

6. Adjust the spray nozzle to make sure it is spraying a fine mist before you light the candle. I turned the nozzle away from the candle to do this. (It isn't a good idea to coat the candle with rubbing alcohol before you try to light it, right?) *Also rinse any alcohol off your hands before lighting the candle.*

7. Light the candle and spray the mist. You should get a nice burst of fire as the mist is ignited by the candle. If you aren't getting a full ball of flame, adjust the placement of the candle until you do. Generally, bending the wire to raise the candle a bit will do the trick.

8. Test it until you get consistent fireballs, and then disassemble the whole thing. If you're working with the guys, they'll enjoy it more if they actually make the flamethrower when you meet.

● **GETTING STARTED**

Have your supplies on a table, and gather the guys together. Have the guys assemble the flamethrower as you explain what they are to do and oversee things.

When the project is complete, ***move the group outside and go over basic safety instructions before putting the rubbing alcohol into the bottle.*** The candle will likely drip wax, so keep that in mind when you pick the spot.

- ***Make sure each guy handling the flamethrower is careful with his aim.*** He needs to watch out for others and for anything around him that may catch fire. If there is a breeze, be sure the guys spray *with* the wind rather than into it, for obvious reasons.

- ***Make sure everyone wears safety goggles.***

- ***Have a bucket filled with water or a garden hose running and handy, just to play it safe.*** You might want to put one of the guys in charge of that.

Important Note: Just before you fill the bottle and light the candle, point out that this *isn't* the type of thing they should try at home, especially if they have younger brothers or sisters around. I'd make them promise. They'll see it as just one more safety guideline and will be quick to agree, but you're really setting up things for your discussion time.

I'd let one of your more responsible guys have the first shot. If he's getting a nice fireball, let him shoot a bit. Guys like fire anyway, and this little torch is almost addicting.

Now, you'll want to get some pictures. Often digital cameras have a bit of a delay in them from the moment you press the shutter release to the instant it captures an image. This makes it really hard to catch the flame burst at its full velocity.

If you have that problem, see if your camera has a "slow synchro" flash setting. With other cameras it may be listed as a "night scene" option, often symbolized with a crescent moon icon. Make the change to the setting, hold the camera *very steady,* and have the person with the flamethrower pump burst after burst as fast as they can. By selecting this mode, the shutter will hang open a bit longer after the flash fires, making it much more likely that you'll catch the full flame effect.

Important Note: If you need to refill the spray bottle, be sure to blow out the candle first.

After everyone has had a turn with the flamethrower, gather the guys together to talk about it. Be sure you put the flamethrower away so it's not a distraction while you're talking together.

● TAKE IT TO THE NEXT LEVEL

You might begin by talking about the flamethrower and how much fun they had with it.

Now can you see why I wanted you to promise not to do this at home, especially if you have younger brothers or sisters around?

What kind of trouble do you think a younger kid could cause with a flamethrower like this, especially if he or she tried it *indoors*?

Try to get them to share some scenarios. If you need to stoke their imagination, ask them more questions. What if they tried it near some sheer drapes? What if they tried to roast marshmallows with it? What if they used it to kill bugs?

If you were to make one of these flamethrowers at home and told your younger brother or sister *not* to touch it (or some neighbor kids who are around), do you think they might still try? Why or why not?

Not all kids would, but let's face it—some would.

What kind of responsibility do you have to younger brothers or sisters, or to other kids in general? If they do something wrong because they saw us do it, what level of blame do we share in that?

| Chinese invented the flamethrower. |

After some discussion, have one of the guys read this aloud:

 "But if you cause one of these little ones who trusts in me to fall into sin, it would be better for you to have a large millstone tied around your neck and be drowned in the depths of the sea. What sorrow awaits the world, because it tempts people to sin. Temptations are inevitable, but what sorrow awaits the person who does the tempting" (Matthew 18:6-7).

What does this verse say about the responsibility you must take for your role in leading a younger person the wrong way?

What are some things that *guys your age* might do that could be a bad example to younger kids?

We're trying to make it easy to share by talking about *other guys* right now. If you need some prompts, here's a short list you may want to refer to:

- Driving fast or recklessly
- Talking disrespectfully to or about parents
- Participating in hidden sins like pornography
- Watching or playing unwholesome movies, songs, or video games
- Not treating girls with honor and respect
- Not spending time with God
- Holding grudges
- Getting even
- Erupting in angry outbursts
- Arguing
- Being selfish—having an "it's all about me" attitude
- Assuming an attitude of superiority
- Indulging in pride
- Putting others down
- Acting dishonestly—compromising your integrity

Listen to Paul's philosophy in 1 Corinthians 10:33–11:1:

 "I, too, try to please everyone in everything I do. I don't just do what is best for me; I do what is best for others so that many may be saved. And you should imitate me, just as I imitate Christ."

Why does Paul feel it is so important to be careful about the kind of example he is? Do you agree or disagree with him? Why?

Paul actually *encourages* us to imitate him. He makes it even clearer in Philippians 4:9:

"Keep putting into practice all you learned and received from me—everything you heard from me and saw me doing. Then the God of peace will be with you."

Do you think you could say this to others—that they should put into practice what they see you doing? Why or why not?

Additional Scriptures: 1 John 2:9-11; 1 Timothy 4:12.

Sum It Up

In light of all this, what type of example do you want to be to others? to those who are younger? weaker? to those who look up to you?

Can you think of one area you want to change—to be a better example in?

What can you do tonight? this week?

They may share verbally, but you may want to give them a few moments of quiet, too. Pray in the end that God will help them.

|⊡| E-MAIL REMINDER (2-3 DAYS LATER)

- Challenge them to strive to be that better example today and tomorrow. Is there something they need to change?
- Attach a digital picture of the flamethrower in action.
- Add a one-line teaser about next week's session.

END CHAPTER FOURTEEN

TIP:
Don't do this devotion if it's windy! Also be sure guys don't spray alcohol on each other.

THEME
Who we are when nobody is looking says a lot about our character and the reality of our faith.

TITLE

C | 15

CHAPTER

Steel Penny Christians

● PREP

You can purchase steel pennies cheaply at a local coin collectors shop or through a dealer over the Internet. I paid 30 cents each for the ones I bought.

Next, borrow or buy a powerful magnet. You'll need one large enough to pick up the entire group of pennies at one time. Check a large hardware store for this. Generally, a magnet sold as a toy *won't* do the job. Remember, a magnet like this can erase memory, so it should be kept away from your computer and other similar electronic devices.

Spread the steel pennies out on a table, and sweep the magnet over them. The magnet should pick them up easily. If not, get a better magnet.

Next, mix the steel pennies and copper ones together, and spread them on the table. Swing the magnet over the top of them again. The magnet should immediately snap up the steel pennies. Perfect. Now practice this one more time in the dark. The magnet should pull the steel pennies even though you can't see what you're doing.

● GETTING STARTED

Sit the guys around a table. Having some kind of food is always a good idea. Keep the magnet close but out of sight initially (maybe in a bag at your feet).

Some of your guys probably haven't seen a steel penny. Start things off by dumping the pile of ordinary copper pennies on the table. Then pass around the steel pennies and ask each of them to take one. They look exactly like the copper pennies of that era, complete with the wheat stalks on the back instead of the Lincoln Memorial like the pennies have today. Hold one up and give them a bit of history on the coin.

During World War II, the United States used copper for bullets, bombs, guns, and shell casings. As supplies ran short, pennies minted in 1943 were made from steel with a thin zinc coating. The combined production of all three government mints (Denver, Philadelphia, and San Francisco) pumped out 1,093,838,670 steel pennies.

The impact for the war effort was significant. I read somewhere that the copper diverted for wartime use was enough to make 1,250,000 shells for the monster field guns. Now, have the guys put the steel pennies back on the table. Mix them

SHOPPING LIST

- large, powerful magnet
- World War II-era steel pennies (1 for you and each guy)
- handful of ordinary copper pennies (at least twice as many as the steel ones)
- scarf or other soft, clean cloth to use as a blindfold
- stopwatch (optional) or watch with a second hand
- digital camera

together with the traditional copper pennies, and ask one of the guys to pick out the steel ones as quickly as he can while you time him. Record his time and repeat this for each of the guys, including yourself.

Now, have them do it again, but this time blindfold each guy before you let him pick out the steel pennies. After being sure he can't see, give him the same number of seconds to find the steel pennies as he took without the blindfold. This would be an ideal time for a picture. Keep a tally of how many steel pennies each guy picks out versus how many copper ones he grabs, and mix the pennies thoroughly between turns. After all the guys have done this, try it yourself. We'll use the magnet soon enough, but keep it out of sight for now.

● TAKE IT TO THE NEXT LEVEL

OK, so picking out all the steel pennies was a sure thing when you weren't wearing the blindfold. On a scale of 1 to 10, with 10 being the most probable, how likely was it that you'd pick out the steel coins 100 percent correctly when you *couldn't* see?

Let's imagine the steel pennies are each of us. The copper pennies are people who are not followers of Christ. Use that scale of 1 to 10 again. How likely is it that other people would consistently identify *you* as a Christian when everyone can see you? The number 10 is absolutely probable (people would always recognize you as a Christian), and the number 1 is least probable (people would never recognize you as a Christian). How do you think these people would rank you?

- parents

- brothers or sisters

- friends from school

- church friends

- youth group leaders

Is it easier to live like a Christian around some people more than others? Explain.

In Joshua 7 we read the sad story of Achan. He was one of the Israelites that made it through a 40-year desert experience. The former generation hadn't trusted God and ended up losing their chance to live in their own country and died in the desert instead. Their kids, Achan's generation, were the faithful ones. They trusted in God and were destined to inherit the land their parents had only dreamed about.

Achan had a family—sons and daughters. But Achan had a secret, too. When nobody was looking, he took something that didn't belong to him and hid it in his tent. Of course, God saw it, and God exposed Achan's cover-up and lies. Achan paid for his secret life with his own life—and the lives of his kids, too.

You can read this whole account in Joshua 7 if you want—but read Joshua 7:24-26 aloud. It's a pretty sad description of what happened to Achan and his family.

Have any of you ever paid a price because someone else wasn't consistently living like a Christian? Can anyone share an example of this?

They've probably seen plenty of this—just as you have. Do you have a story *you* can share if they don't? Mistreated by a Christian boss? Slandered by another Christian, or whatever? If you share your story, it might be a good idea to leave out the real names of the people involved—this isn't a time to gossip, but a time to express that even people who are Christians aren't always living as God planned.

So which Achan was the real Achan? The man he was in public or the man he was when nobody was looking?

Think about this next question—but don't answer out loud. What if nobody could see you? *Nobody.* **How consistently would you be in living as you know God would want you to live?**

What if you had a ring, like Frodo in *The Lord of the Rings,* that gave you the power to disappear? Would you still live like a follower of Christ when nobody could see you?

Let me put it another way. Do you do the same things in broad daylight that you do under the cover of darkness? You're in your room at night. You're home alone on the computer. Whatever. Are you more likely to live like a Christian when nobody is watching, or less likely? Rank it from 1 to 10 again. How does your score compare?

Guys may be uncomfortable sharing at this point. That's OK. Just let them think on it and rank themselves silently.

If you're less likely to live like a Christian when nobody can see you, then which person is the *real* you?

Who you are in the dark is who you are.

Agree or disagree: The dark reveals our true character more than the light. Explain your answer.

Now, tell them that you're going to put the blindfold on and that you're confident you'll find every steel penny in the pile in as fast a time as you did *without* the blindfold. And you won't pick up one copper penny either.

They won't believe you, or they will know you have some kind of trick up your sleeve. You might tell them you can teach any one of them the technique in less than 10 seconds. They'll really want to see you prove all this.

After the blindfold is in place, whip the magnet out of the bag, and with your other hand to guide you around the pile of pennies, swing the magnet over the top. Presto! You'll have your pennies—plus a lot of complaints that you cheated or that this wasn't fair. Nice job!

You can imagine that some of the guys may want to see the magnet or try it themselves. I'd try to wait until after you're done to let them do that so you don't totally lose the momentum you have going.

Sum It Up

Whether you're blindfolded or not, whether you're in the dark or in the light, the magnet quickly picks up the steel pennies. The results are exactly the same. That's the way it needs to be with us. We need to be consistent.

Whether we're out in plain sight, or in the privacy of our own room, we should be like "steel penny" Christians—consistent and easily identifiable. If we aren't, we'll likely hurt ourselves and others. Listen to this verse:

 "What sorrow awaits those who try to hide their plans from the Lord, who do their evil deeds in the dark! 'The Lord can't see us,' they say. 'He doesn't know what's going on!' " (Isaiah 29:15)

Is there something in your life that needs to change? Does the way you live depend on if someone is watching or not? The way I see it, we can either try harder to cover it up or ask God to help us change.

Achan tried to cover it up. He proved he could fool others, and maybe himself, *but not God.* I urge you to deal with any inconsistencies in your life.

Have one of the guys read this verse aloud:

 "But don't just listen to God's word. You must do what it says. Otherwise, you are only fooling yourselves. For if you listen to the word and don't obey, it is like glancing at your face in a mirror. You see yourself, walk away, and forget what you look like. But if you look carefully into the perfect law that sets you free, and if you do what it says and don't forget what you heard, then God will bless you for doing it" (James 1:22-25).

If you have time, talk with the guys about the freedom we find when we follow God's Word consistently. Pray that they'll take this to heart.

Finally, give them each a steel penny to keep as a reminder of the kind of consistent Christian we truly ought to be—even in the dark.

▯ **E-MAIL REMINDER (2-3 DAYS LATER)**

- Type out James 1:22-25 and Ephesians 5:8, 11.
- Ask if they put the steel penny someplace where it will serve as a reminder to be consistent as a Christian, whether they're all alone or in public.
- Remind them that you're available to talk anytime. Add your cellphone number.
- Add a one-line teaser about next week's lesson, and invite them out.
- Attach digital photos.

END CHAPTER FIFTEEN

TIP:
Just for fun, see how many things you can buy with your leftover pennies.

THEME

Honoring our parents is something God expects and rewards.

TITLE

Gravity and Other Guarantees

c | 16

CHAPTER

● PREP

The easiest place to find the three-man water balloon launcher is online. You'll want to start working on this right away to allow for shipping time. Search using the phrase "water balloon slingshots" and you should have a wide selection for a variety of prices.

Small balloons work best. Fill them to about the size of an orange. You'll need two other people to help you practice the slingshot. Be sure to pick an outdoor place to try this with plenty of room, and make sure everyone wears safety glasses.

Directions should come with the launcher, but basically think of an old-fashioned "Y-shaped" slingshot. Two people stand about 4 feet apart and each holds one end of the slingshot with outstretched arms. The third person grabs the pouch dangling between them at the end of the rubber tubing. This person loads the balloon in the pouch and stretches the hosing back as far as he can. When released, the balloon may catapult hundreds of feet. A little practice will give you a feel for how much room you'll actually need.

Be thinking about how you want to do this with the guys. Here are some ideas to keep them really engaged:

- Give an award for the longest shot.

- Award the team that gets closest to a target.

- *Wearing safety goggles,* volunteers stand in the field with large garbage cans (all three guys from a team would hold one) or 5-gallon buckets to try to catch the balloons the shooting team launches. A catch could give the shooting team an "out" or give the catching team a point.

One last thing. Depending on where you do this with the guys, you'll have to think about water availability. You may need to fill the balloons in advance.

● GETTING STARTED

When the guys get together, put them all on water-balloon-filling detail. If you brought garbage cans or buckets, you can use them to hold the filled balloons. Laundry baskets also work well. When you think you've filled enough balloons, keep filling even more. You'll go through these fast.

After you form three-man teams, start the water-balloon barrage. Beginning with a simple distance or target competition is

RISK

LOW   MED   HI

SHOPPING LIST

- small balloons (for water balloons)

- 3-man water balloon launcher (the giant slingshot type)

- safety goggles

- 2 or more full-size plastic garbage barrels or 5-gallon buckets

- paper and pen for each guy

- digital camera

good. After every team has had a round, move to one of the other options if you want. Also, let guys rotate positions on their teams so that different guys do the launching while taking turns holding the slingshot.

Keep your notes or Bible in a dry spot, because I'd expect the guys may resort to a little "hand-to-hand" combat and water balloons will be bursting everywhere. Don't forget to capture some digital pictures.

When the balloon bombardment is over, send the guys out to pick up the scraps and toss them out. Even if you're out in a forest preserve, you don't want to take a chance that a child may put a piece in his or her mouth.

● TAKE IT TO THE NEXT LEVEL

Get the guys together and start out something like this:

When you were launching the water balloons, what physical "law" did it illustrate?

You may get a variety of answers, but "gravity" is what you're looking for.

No matter how high or far you hurled them, the water balloons always came down. The law of gravity is an absolute. If you send a water balloon in the air, it will come back down again, guaranteed.

We want to talk about another kind of absolute—another kind of guarantee that we find in the Bible.

Read these verses aloud, or have one of the guys read them aloud:

 "Children, obey your parents because you belong to the Lord, for this is the right thing to do. 'Honor your father and mother.' This is the first commandment with a promise: If you honor your father and mother, 'things will go well for you, and you will have a long life on the earth' " (Ephesians 6:1-3).

"Honor your father and mother." This is part of the Ten Commandments and is recorded in Exodus 20:12 and Deuteronomy 5:16.

What are the promises or guarantees that come with honoring parents?

Things will go well with you. A long life.

List some ways we can honor our parents. I'd like each of you to write down every suggestion that's made.

Take your time with this question and the next one. This is where the bulk of the spade work needs to be done in this session. Jot the things down as they share as well. Make a list yourself ahead of time so you can use it to prompt the guys if they run out of ideas too early. If you don't have kids of your own, talk to some parents and get feedback. You'll have plenty of material. Here's a list I made. You may want to pick one or more of these and dig in a little deeper to really help them understand.

- Obey, listen, and talk kindly to parents, and show respect for them in words and actions—even when they aren't around. Learn to communicate without arguing, accept their rules and guidelines without grumbling, and don't complain about your parents to friends.

- Appreciate parents and show it. Thank them for things they do for you—even the routine things—and the different ways they provide and sacrifice for you.

- Fill them in on the details of your life, talk to them about your dreams, tell them about the girl you like and why, and ask their advice and value it.

- Treat them like they matter to you, live in a way that will make them proud, spend time with them, show initiative, be industrious, and develop integrity.

- Think. Exercise good judgment, and be responsible.

OK, so I wrote a lot of things down, but these are the kinds of things you can prompt them with if they run out of ideas themselves.

List some ways we might *dishonor* parents. Everybody keep a list of all the ideas here, too.

Obviously, these will be the opposite of many of those things listed above. Also skim through Proverbs for more ideas. See Proverbs 10:1, 5; 15:5; 17:25; and 19:13.

How do you think God would want us to treat parents who don't *deserve* to be honored?

After the guys share some opinions, read Ephesians 6:1-3 again.

Do these verses say anything about honoring parents only when they deserve it? Why do you think that is?

What if parents are abusing their kids—how can we honor them?

Tough question, but you need to address it. We honor our parents by doing the right thing—even if that right thing means taking measures to protect yourself physically or going to the authorities for help. The guys need to understand that allowing abuse to continue doesn't honor an abusive parent—it enables them to do something that is harmful to themselves and others.

What if parents ask you to do something that conflicts with your convictions as a follower of Christ?

We need to obey God rather than men (Acts 5:29), but we must be very careful with this. It's easy to get self-righteous. Usually, a creative alternative can be suggested that everyone feels comfortable with.

What about a stepparent? Are you obligated to honor them?

Depending on the makeup of your group, you may want to address this. If Ephesians 6:1-3 only applies to biological parents, what would you say about guys who were adopted?

What about single-parent homes? Or what if my parents don't get along? How can I honor them when they're at war with each other?

Look at the list of ways to honor a parent again. Wouldn't many of those still work?

What about the whole "things will go well for you" guarantee? What kinds of things might this be referring to?

Can you give any examples of guys you know who usually honor their parents and those who don't?

Be ready with some examples yourself. How were you at their age? If you did honor your parents, how did that work out well for you over the long haul? If you didn't honor your parents, what type of regrets are you shouldering? Would you do it differently if you could?

Sum It Up

No matter what your situation, you can find ways to honor your parents more. Would you agree with that? Why or why not?

Like the law of gravity, "what goes up must come down," honoring our parents has its own law. Honor your mom and dad, and it will go well with you. It's the old principle, "what goes around comes around."

Each of you is accountable to God for how you treat your parents, just like they're accountable to God for how they treat you.

Wouldn't you rather be in a position where God promises to make things go well for you instead of learning the hard way all the time?

Have guys look at the list they wrote of ways to honor their parents and circle some that they'd like to work on beginning now.

Then have guys look at the list of things they wrote that dishonor parents and put an X through ones they don't want to do anymore—beginning now.

Encourage guys to take the list home and review it regularly. Perhaps they can even evaluate themselves every day for a week or two. Also encourage them to pray and ask God for help with this.

Close by reading Proverbs 23:22-25.

|◻| **E-MAIL REMINDER (2-3 DAYS LATER)**

- Briefly recap the importance of honoring our parents. Be sure to include the guarantee—the promise.
- Type out Ephesians 6:1-3 and possibly Proverbs 23:22-25.
- Remind them to review their lists of ways to honor/dishonor parents.
- Attach a digital picture of a water balloon launching.
- Add a one-line teaser about next week's session.

TIP:
Did you remember to pick up all the balloon pieces?

END CHAPTER SIXTEEN

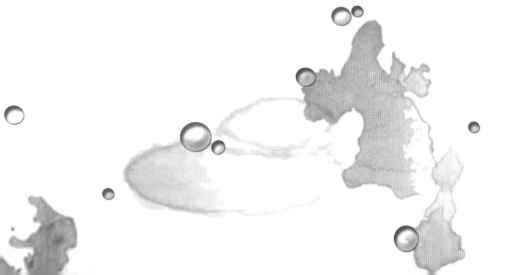

C | 17

CHAPTER

TITLE
Wrecking Yard

RISK

LOW　　MED　　HI

SHOPPING LIST

- Locate an auto body repair shop or auto wrecker's yard to visit.
- digital camera

● PREP

You'll need to do a little phone calling and legwork to be fully prepared for the guys. The plan is to take them to see some wrecked autos at either an auto body repair shop or an auto wrecker. You can find locations for either by checking the yellow pages section of your local phone directory.

There's something powerful about actually *seeing* mangled cars rather than shortcutting the visual end of this by simply *talking* about it. After visiting the wrecks personally, you may want to search an online used-car dealer to find a picture of some of the same makes and models you saw at the wrecking yard to print out for the guys as a little "before and after" comparison.

Also, try to get some real live car accident stories from your past or people you know. Of particular importance is what *caused* the accident. If you have any pictures you can show—even better!

Finally, gather up a story or two about guys who messed up their lives or nearly did because of something they did even though they knew better. Maybe it's your story or something that happened to a guy you know.

● GETTING STARTED

Bring the guys out to the wrecked cars. Let them see the crystals of windshield glass strewn across the interior. Have them touch the crumpled metal. Encourage them to check out the buckled seat or deflated air bag.

Go over the cars like a crime scene investigation crew. Have them speculate how the accident happened. Toss out scenarios about how the driver got into this mess. Talking on a cellphone? Driving under the influence of drugs or alcohol? Goofing around with a passenger? Trying to pick up a dropped french fry?

Some guys may take this seriously, while others may make a joke out of everything. Either reaction will work fine, so roll with whatever mood they're in. Take a picture of the guys with each car you inspect.

Take note of where the damage is. Was it a head-on collision—something the driver should have seen coming but for some reason couldn't avoid? Did the driver get rear-ended? Maybe he or she was blindsided in some way? There may even be someone working there who can tell you how the accidents happened.

Finally, with each wreck you inspect, get the guys to give their assessment on the condition of the driver after the accident. What's their verdict? Did the driver make it? Suppose there were passengers. Would they have survived? How about any other car involved? What might have been the extent of those injuries?

● TAKE IT TO THE NEXT LEVEL

Now, move to a place you can talk with the guys. A fast-food restaurant is generally a good idea. Fuel the guys up with a soft drink and fries, and start your discussion.

Let's start out with an obvious question. Out of all the wrecked cars we saw, how many of them do you think were deliberately wrecked? How many of those drivers did something intentionally, knowing it would end up wrecking his car?

We want to establish the fact that none of the drivers wanted things to end up the way they did.

That's why they call them *accidents*. Now, let's just take a guess on something. What percentage of the drivers were 100 percent innocent in the accident? They were alert, driving defensively. Their reaction time was perfect.

You can also add some of these conditions:

- *They weren't speeding.*

- *They weren't talking on a cellphone.*

- *They weren't drowsy.*

- *They weren't inattentive in any way—like eating, adjusting the radio, looking at a billboard, or whatever.*

- *They were totally obeying the traffic rules and signals.*

In other words, what percentage do you think had absolutely *no fault* in causing or contributing to the accident in any way?

What percentage may have been able to avoid the accident, or maybe have lessoned its effect if they'd been more on guard, more alert?

Generally, they will concede that some accidents may have been prevented this way.

Anybody have a story they want to share about an accident you saw or that somebody you know was involved in? What happened? Whose fault was it?

Allow some time for stories. Share one of your own here if you have one.

The same thing can happen to us. Imagine we're the drivers and the car is life. How do some guys end up making a wreck of their lives?

Let them make a list of things. Bad habits. Compromising standards. Letting themselves be influenced by wrong friends. Poor choices.

Think about the wrecked cars we saw for a moment. Take a guess. What percentage of these drivers were licensed drivers versus driving with a permit with a licensed driver sitting beside them?

Pretty safe to assume most were licensed, seasoned vets.

Why is it there are more accidents involving qualified, licensed drivers—drivers who've been given the stamp of approval to drive on their own?

How often do you think carelessness becomes a factor? or about having a relaxed attitude about driving this machine weighing thousands of pounds at high speeds?

How can this happen to us in life, too?

How might we get careless about our choices as we get a little older and become more independent from our parents?

We forget the dangers of life. We let down our guard. We drive "fast" and do things our parents wouldn't approve of if they knew.

If you have a story you can share of someone who did just that, now's a great time to share it.

Think about college life for a moment. How do some guys end up making a wreck of their lives when they get totally away from home? Why do you think that happens?

Talk about that for a few minutes. The more independent we are from the watchful eye of parents, the greater our risk may be for lapsing into bad habits or practices if we're not careful.

Here are some ways you might mention:

- Some drift away from God and their faith.

- Some become obsessed with things they should avoid.

- Some make the wrong friends and have bad influences in their lives.

Let's look at a few driving basics and relate them to our lives. Here are three things that make us safer drivers and will keep us safer on the road of life as well:

1. A good driver follows the rules. Speed limits. Safety belts. When he starts pushing the limits, running the red lights—he's asking for trouble. What are rules you think we should be following in life? Why do you think those rules are the best ones?

| Ernest Holmes was the inventor of the tow truck in 1916. |

Determine to follow the principles of God's Word and the things our parents taught us. These things are all for our safety. Unless we dedicate ourselves to these convictions, we'll likely stray.

 "How can a young person stay pure? By obeying your word" (Psalm 119:9).

2. A good driver drives defensively. He checks his mirrors. He stays aware of the potential dangers around him. How can we do that?

Never forget life is dangerous. It's more of a demolition derby than anything. The devil targets us—and all too often we are easy prey when we get out of the house. We have to stay alert to the dangers and ask God to help us daily. Check out 1 Corinthians 16:13:

 "Be on guard. Stand firm in the faith. Be courageous. Be strong."

3. A good driver doesn't allow others to distract him. How can we do that?

Be careful who you choose to hang out with and of the influence they have on you. Remember how 1 Corinthians 15:33 warns us that "bad company corrupts good character."

 "My child, if sinners entice you, turn your back on them!" (Proverbs 1:10)

 "Of course, your former friends are surprised when you no longer plunge into the flood of wild and destructive things they do. So they slander you. But remember that they will have to face God, who will judge everyone, both the living and the dead" (1 Peter 4:4-5).

Sum It Up

As you get older, it's only natural that you're given more independence. By the time you go to college, you'll have the freedom to make practically all your choices—good or bad.

This is a time of testing—make no mistake about it.

Many end up disregarding the basics—the rules of the road they were raised on. They ignore the basic principles from God's Word—the very things that are there for our happiness and protection. *They put themselves on a collision course with danger.*

When someone gets hurt, crippled, or killed in an accident, how many other people are affected?

Think about this for a moment. An accident can change many lives—even the lives of those who are not in the car. Help guys draw the connection between what happens in a car accident because of the driver's choices and what happens in life because of our choices. How do those choices affect others?

If a person is fortunate enough to survive a wreck, he can always get a new car. In life it isn't that simple. Sometimes you have to live with the effects of that wreck the rest of your life.

TIP:
Be sure to thank the person who works at the wrecking yard for his or her help.

Do remind guys that God is always willing to forgive—but even with forgiveness we often have consequences for our actions.

Let me read you a verse written by someone who seemed to understand the dangers of life, especially when one is out on his or her own. This is like a prayer—one which each of you may want to pray in your own heart.

 "Your instructions are more valuable to me than millions in gold and silver. You made me; you created me. Now give me the sense to follow your commands" (Psalm 119:72-73).

E-MAIL REMINDER (2-3 DAYS LATER)

- Briefly recap the point of the lesson in a few lines.
- Encourage them to commit to follow God's principles and avoid a potential wreck.
- Add a one-liner to whet their appetite for next week's session.
- Attach a digital photo of the guys with the wrecked cars.

END CHAPTER SEVENTEEN

THEME
Absolute truth exists, and we can find it in God's Word.

TITLE
The Right Combination

● PREP

Purchase combination locks and remove them from the packaging. Keep a master list of the combinations and corresponding serial numbers of the locks so you don't get mixed up. Also, select one lock that you'll keep on you and *memorize* the combination.

Finally, jot down a series of bogus combinations on separate pieces of paper—one for each of the guys.

● GETTING STARTED

Get the guys together and hand out the combination locks—but don't give them the combinations. Keep your lock put away for now. Explain that the whole group will get pizza next time if any one of them opens his combination lock successfully.

Suggest they try the locker combination they use at school. When that doesn't work, ask them to make up a combination or try some sequence of numbers that is meaningful to them—like their birthday.

Some guys may see this as a no-win situation and may slouch in their chairs without trying. Encourage them to try harder.

After a minute or two—as you see some of them thinking the whole exercise is futile—hand out the pieces of paper with the phony combinations. Ask them to try again.

As you see them failing, advise them to switch combinations with the guy next to them, and then switch again if that doesn't work. Encourage them to concentrate. Try harder. Believe.

Pull out your lock while they're all busy with theirs. Say something about them making this a lot harder than it really is. You'll want to get their attention a bit so they look up at you.

Ask someone to shout out his combination. Then ask him to repeat it slowly, one number at a time. As he gives you the number, you're *really* dialing the combination you memorized. When you casually open the lock—they'll probably be surprised.

Snap the lock closed and toss it to the guy who gave you the combination. Ask him to do it now—*for the pizza.* The other guys should be watching now, and they'll be just as frustrated as he is when he doesn't get it.

Advise him to concentrate—ask the others to be quiet—and have him try again. After he fails, you might ask to see the lock and have him call out the combination again. Once again, you're really using the combination you memorized earlier. After you open it nonchalantly, their frustration will mount.

RISK

LOW   MED   HI

SHOPPING LIST

- combination lock for each of the guys and 1 for yourself
- digital camera

Maybe give one last chance for the pizza. See if someone else wants to try the lock you just opened. Someone will likely volunteer—but of course, they'll fail, too.

Now, calm the guys down and make some sense of all this.

● TAKE IT TO THE NEXT LEVEL

OK, tell me what the problem was. Why couldn't any of you open the locks?

Clearly, they didn't have the right combination.

Did it make a difference when you tried *really hard* to *believe* the lock would open? Did you find that trying harder actually helped? Why not?

To open the lock properly (not cutting it), you need the right combination. Would everyone agree in the absolute truth of that statement?

Do you think most other people would agree with that, too?

Strangely enough, many people say "absolute truth" really doesn't exist anymore. They believe what's true for *you* may not be true for *them.*

If you're talking about *preferences,* my "truth" may indeed be different from yours. My favorite dinner may be spaghetti. That's the absolute truth. Yours may be steak. And that's the absolute truth. Right? In a case like this, absolute truth is different for each of us based on our preferences.

There are other areas of life where absolute truth is immovable. It doesn't change, regardless of a person's preferences or points of view. Can you name some?

Laws of nature are absolute truth. Gravity. Speed of light.

People accept these areas of absolute truth—yet many don't want to believe God's Word contains absolute truth. For example, they don't believe John 14:6 where Jesus states, "I am the way, the truth, and the life. No one can come to the Father except through me." They insist there are many ways to heaven. Why do you suppose they want to believe the Bible isn't "absolute truth"?

Why do you suppose people want to believe there is more than one way to heaven?

Just because somebody *sincerely believes* their works will get them into heaven, does that make it true? Why or why not?

People can be sincere, but they can be sincerely wrong. Truth is truth, whether you believe it or not. You might believe *any* sequence of numbers will open the combination lock, *but that doesn't change the truth.*

| Only experts can distinguish between the three or more false gates and the true gate, and, since a lock with four discs can use any of 100,000,000 possible combinations, identifying the correct one by chance is unlikely. |

When we use a combination lock, we have to be careful to dial the right numbers so the lock opens for us. How hard is it to unlock the truth from the Bible?

Sometimes it's relatively easy—other times it can seem hard.

Unlike these combination locks, the Bible doesn't come with a three-step combination for unlocking each of its truths. It's almost like we have to be a lock picker sometimes. We've all seen guys pick a lock on a big bank vault in movies. What are some of the things they need to pick a lock?

Things they might mention are a teacher or mentor, tools, time, training, patience, and so on. For each of these, encourage them to consider an equivalent for "unlocking" the truths of the Bible. Here are some helps for you:

TIP:
For fun, you can have the guys try to "pick" their locks at this point. See if they can hear the clicks in the mechanism and figure out the combination. Don't spend too long on this, but it's a fun way to lead into this part of the discussion. Or you might show a movie clip of a guy picking a lock in a heist movie.

- Training: This might relate to going to church, being involved in a Bible study, or taking other classes to help them learn. This might also be books or magazine articles.

- Teacher or mentor: This could be a relationship with a more mature Christian. Perhaps it's a pastor, youth leader, parent, or older friend who's a little further down the road in his faith and who can help a guy find answers to his questions.

- Tools: This might be other study tools such as concordances, books, Bible study guides, and so on.

- Practice: The more we read the Bible, the better we are at understanding it. We find verses that relate to other passages we've recently read.

- Quiet: In the movies, the lock pickers want to be free from distractions. You might even show a movie clip of a guy picking a lock. He always has everyone be quiet so he can listen and concentrate. We might need to find some time that's quiet (maybe even turn off the music!) so we can concentrate on the Bible and what God's telling us.

- Patience and time: Well…we all need those!

What ultimate mentor has God provided for us? Listen to this verse:

 "But when the Father sends the Advocate as my representative— that is, the Holy Spirit—he will teach you everything and will remind you of everything I have told you" (John 14:26).

How does the Holy Spirit teach us? How do you feel about having the ultimate mentor help you understand the truth?

Here's something else to think about. A lock picker can't open the lock with just part of the combination. He needs the whole thing. Let me read you another verse here:

"Work hard so you can present yourself to God and receive his approval. Be a good worker, one who does not need to be ashamed and who correctly explains the word of truth" (2 Timothy 2:15).

This says "correctly explains the word of truth." Do you think people can explain the Bible incorrectly? Can they twist the truth? If so, how?

This might include pulling a verse out without getting the whole sequence or without making sure we understand the context, or mixing traditions with truth and blurring the lines of what is really true and what is a matter of tradition or preference.

Make sure they get this. It's really important. Stripping one verse out of context can lead to wrong interpretations.

How can that get us in trouble? How can that be dangerous? How can that destroy our faith?

This might be a time to share a story of how someone was turned away from God because of the truth being twisted and presented incorrectly.

Sum It Up

In our culture and world, some people want to believe that "truth" can mean anything they decide it should mean. Buying into that flawed thinking will hurt us because the universe doesn't operate that way.

"Absolute truth" exists, and we can find it in God's Word. And understanding a Scripture passage is as essential as getting the series of numbers right to open a combination lock.

We want to get skilled at unlocking the truths of the Bible like safecrackers get really good at opening locks. How can we do this?

Help them put it all together. Review some of the ideas shared earlier, and also include prayer.

Be sensitive, be listening to what the Spirit is trying to tell you. Ask God to show you. Make it your prayer.

 "Open my eyes to see the wonderful truths in your instructions" (Psalm 119:18).

Many well-meaning people will try to convince you that there are no absolute truths. They'll admit there's only one combination for a silly lock, but they refuse to think that the God of the universe may have a specific set of principles for us to live by, or that he would provide only one way to heaven, for example.

We live in a world of lies and deception. I want to encourage you to seek God's truth in his Word every day. Will you do that?

I'd like each of you to keep your combination lock. See me afterward and I'll give you the correct combination. Whenever you see your lock, remember that there is absolute truth and that you'll find it in God's Word.

Take a picture of the guys as a group holding up their locks.

|☐| E-MAIL REMINDER (2-3 DAYS LATER)

- Sum up the main idea of the lesson in a few sentences.
- Remind them to find truth in the Bible, and encourage them to start today if they aren't already doing it.
- Add a one-line teaser about next week's lesson.
- Attach the digital picture of the guys with their locks.

END CHAPTER EIGHTEEN

TIP:
You may want to have guys mark their locks so they don't get mixed up.

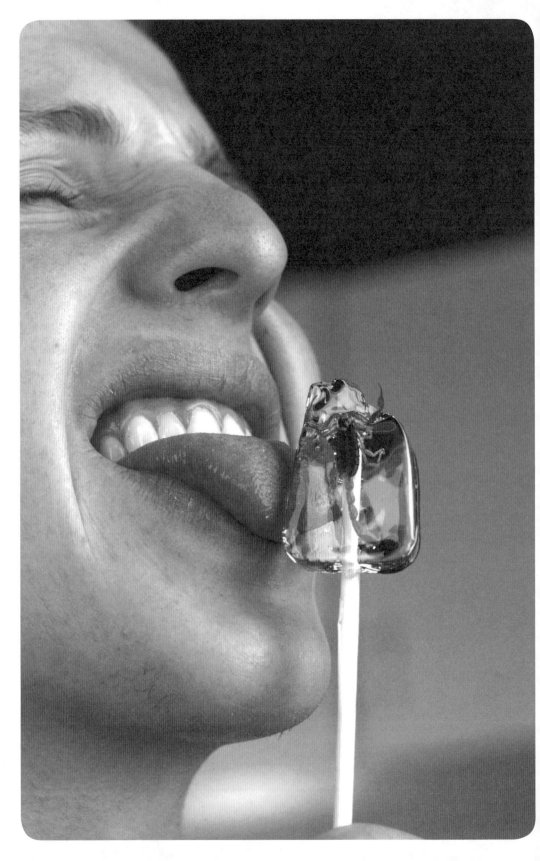

THEME
Making choices based simply on our own viewpoints and the opinions of those who see things the same way we do can be dangerous.

TITLE

C | 19
CHAPTER

Defective Perspective

● PREP

Using several different examples, you'll show the guys how limiting themselves to their own viewpoints, or those of like-minded friends, can lead to bad choices. Let's go over exactly what you're going to do.

RISK

LOW   MED   HI

- **Black Light Example**—Experiment with illuminating your clothing using a black light in a dark room. Using a different light like this will change how everything you're wearing looks. Now shake some baby powder on your pants. In daylight or under traditional lighting, the powder will appear white. Under the black light, you'd expect the powder to look purple but it looks *black*.

You can usually find black lights at teacher supply stores, party supply stores, or online.

SHOPPING LIST

- black light—18-inch fluorescent tube type or a light bulb
- baby powder
- medical advertisement (try *Reader's Digest* magazine)
- scorpion suckers (1 for each guy—see notes in Prep section)
- digital camera

- **Advertisement Example**—Pick up a magazine and thumb through it to find a medical advertisement. The general format usually includes an appealing picture and benefit statement on the first page followed by one or more pages of impossibly fine print describing possible side effects. When you find just the right ad, you'll be able to illustrate how a closer look will often give you a different perspective.

The ad I chose describes a wonderful-sounding medication to help you sleep at night. A quick glance at the following pages revealed some "special concerns," as the ad termed it. One concern was that the medication may cause "sleep driving," which is just like sleepwalking only patients get out of bed and go for drives—while still asleep. Other concerns listed are "strange behavior," hallucinations, and suicidal thoughts. I think I'll sleep a whole lot better just knowing I *didn't* try this product.

- **Scorpion Suckers**—Pick up a sucker for each of the guys. These things look nasty. Picture a small candy lollipop with a whole scorpion visible in the center. For some reason museum gift shops often have these. You can also find them at some candy shops, and they're available online, too. I've been assured the suckers are safe to eat. The suckers with scorpions inside are the most dramatic option for this session, but you can also buy suckers with crickets or worms inside.

When you get the candy, you'll notice one side has a sticker on it describing the contents. Use a permanent marker to block out the words "Scorpion Sucker" so you're ready for the guys. This way, when you look at it from one angle, all you see is the harmless label. The scorpion will be visible only when you turn the sucker completely around.

● GETTING STARTED

Get the guys together in a room you can completely darken.

Turn off all the lights in the room, and have the guys observe how different the colors in their clothes look with the black light. Be sure they see how white looks purple. You may even want to pass the light around. If you're sitting around a table with food—which I highly suggest—sweep the black light over the food to see the change in how things look. After a minute or two of this, turn the room lights back on and ask them to share the differences they observed.

Now shake some baby powder on your pants. Based on what they just saw about the black light, what color do they suppose the powder will appear in the purple glow of the black light? They'll probably guess purple. Turn off the room lights to show them. The powder appears *black*.

● TAKE IT TO THE NEXT LEVEL

We've all seen the effects of black lights before—but were any of you surprised that the white powder appeared black instead of purple? Did anything else look different than you expected it would look? If so, what?

The thing is, when we view something in a different light, things can look very different from what we might expect.

Hold up the medicine ad for all of them to see. Just show the front part of the ad. Read some of the advertising copy describing the benefits of the medicine. Point out the ad's use of color, graphics, or maybe the nice photo with smiling, happy people.

What kind of mood is this creating? How does it make you feel about the product being advertised, or the people who use the product?

If you were experiencing the problem described here, might this ad make you interested in trying the product? Why or why not?

Now flip the page and start reading some of the warnings, disclaimers, and potential side effects.

How does hearing some of the specific downsides to the medicine make you feel about trying the product now?

When we look a little closer, we find some things look a whole lot different than they did on the surface. Can you think of any

| Scientists aren't sure why, but scorpions are fluorescent under ultraviolet light. |

examples of a time your perspective on something totally changed when you got the whole story?

Maybe you have a story you can share here about yourself or someone you know.

In the Bible there's a tragic story of King Solomon's son Rehoboam. It's told in 1 Kings 12. Solomon had died and the people of Israel gathered to crown Rehoboam as their king.

The people told Rehoboam that his father made things very difficult for them. They told him that they'd serve him as king as long as he made things a bit easier for them.

Rehoboam asked them to return for his answer in three days. In that time he got input from two different groups. First, he consulted with his father's advisers. Being older, these men had seen and experienced many things. They advised Rehoboam to listen to the people because the people were right. They urged Rehoboam to speak kindly to the people and assure them he would make life easier for them. If he did, these older men believed the people would be loyal to Rehoboam forever.

Make things easier for the people? Rehoboam didn't like their advice one bit.

So he got opinions from some of his *friends.* Guys he'd grown up with. Their perspective matched Rehoboam's. They counseled him to talk tough to the people and tell them he would make things *harder* on them, not easier.

Rehoboam *liked* that advice, and when the people gathered at the appointed time, he told them how rough he was going to make things for them. It seemed he intended to scare them into obeying him.

But the people rebelled. Eleven of the 12 tribes (or groups) of Israel walked out. Only one tribe made Rehoboam its king.

Rehoboam refused to see things from any other perspective than his own—and he lost most of his kingdom as a result. He lost *big.*

Do we ever do that? Do we ever get counsel and input from friends our own age who share our perspective? Do we even bother to ask parents for advice?

Some of you may be thinking, "I already know what my parents would say." Since you don't like what you think they're going to say, you avoid it altogether by not even trying to get their input.

Rehoboam's dad, Solomon, wrote something before he died. It says:

 "Without wise leadership, a nation falls; there is safety in having many advisers" (Proverbs 11:14).

Too bad Rehoboam didn't take his dad's advice either.

Encourage guys to share who they're most likely to go to for advice, and why they've chosen those people.

Then read Proverbs 15:22:

 "Plans go wrong for lack of advice; many advisers bring success."

What do you think this verse means for you?

Is getting advice from people you think will always agree with you really getting advice? Why or why not?

Sum It Up

It's true, parents and other adults *don't* always see things the same way you do.

That's what makes their input so valuable.

How is the advice of parents like or unlike the black light?

How is it like or unlike the medicine ad?

Ultimately, God wants us to come to him for advice and counsel.

 "Trust in the Lord with all your heart; do not depend on your own understanding. Seek his will in all you do, and he will show you which path to take. Don't be impressed with your own wisdom" (Proverbs 3:5-7a).

Hold up one of the suckers with the label facing the guys so they can't see the surprise inside.

This sucker was pretty expensive as suckers go.

Tell the guys how much it cost—just to show it's valuable.

Let's look at it from a different angle.

Turn the sucker around so the scorpion is visible.

I'd like each of you to have one of these suckers. I don't expect you to eat it but just to keep it around as a reminder of the need to get different perspectives, like from our parents and from God, before we act or make decisions.

If you have time, share one more verse:

 "There is a path before each person that seems right, but it ends in death" (Proverbs 14:12).

Going it on our own or getting advice only from our friends can give us a defective perspective—and that's dangerous.

Instead, seek God before you act or make decisions. Get input from your parents and people older and wiser than your friends. You'll gain an effective perspective that will be much more likely to keep you safe and bring you success.

Take a group photo with the guys and the suckers.

|▢| E-MAIL REMINDER (2-3 DAYS LATER)

- Summarize the main points of the session in just a few lines.
- Remind them to seek input from parents; God; and older, wiser, or more experienced people to gain an effective perspective.
- Add a one-line teaser inviting them to next week's session.
- Attach a digital picture.

END CHAPTER NINETEEN

TIP:
Just curious. Did you eat one of the scorpions?

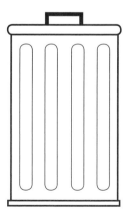

THEME
Dating a non-Christian may seem harmless enough, but it is filled with many dangers and will likely lead only to heartache and ruin.

TITLE
The Three-legged Race Case

RISK

LOW   MED   HI

SHOPPING LIST

• duct tape or scarf to tie legs together

• location and items to use for an obstacle course

• stopwatch or watch with a second hand

• digital camera

● **PREP**

The guys will be running a three-legged obstacle course race, so you'll need to have something to hold their legs together securely. An elastic bandage, a scarf...even duct tape should work. Try to experiment with this ahead of time to see what works well. *Do note, if guys are wearing shorts, don't use duct tape!*

After you figure out where to set up, make the course difficult for them to maneuver. Set up chairs, benches, or other things for them to weave around. Old tires from a tire store work great, too. If you have a playground that you can use, that can add fun elements, too (just be sure you're not knocking over small children while doing this!).

If you line up the rows of tires (three across) for them to hop through like an agility drill, you're likely to see teams fall onto the tires before they get very far. That will tie in nicely during your discussion time.

● **GETTING STARTED**

Set up your obstacle course before the guys arrive. Have them pick a partner for a three-legged race through the obstacle course, and run one pair at a time. With the partners facing the same direction and standing shoulder to shoulder, tie their inside legs together. Time each team as they run the course, and record it.

When everyone has had a turn, explain that you'd like each team to do it again—but a little differently. This time, one of them has to be facing *backward* while the other is facing *forward* when they're tied together. Be sure that you're out there with the camera and that you record each team's time. When the last team finishes, gather the guys together for discussion.

● **TAKE IT TO THE NEXT LEVEL**

Start by reading aloud the comparison of each pair's times for the two heats. There should be a marked difference in their scores— and if you made the course difficult enough, there will be.

What were the differences between the two ways we ran the race? What were the challenges of each way of running it?

If you were running this as a marathon for a cash prize—say a million dollars—and maybe anyone who lost had to pay a penalty of $10,000, which way would you run the race? Can you imagine

anybody in their right mind risking losing so much by choosing to face in opposite directions?

Some of the guys may say that's exactly what they'd do. Don't let that rattle you. You can be sure they're tracking with you.

There's another marathon event in life that's similar to a three-legged race in many ways. Only this event doesn't just last 26 miles. It lasts a lifetime. I'm talking about marriage. How is marriage like or unlike being tied to someone in a marathon three-legged race over rough terrain?

Marriage means two different people joined together for the long haul. Sometimes there may be chafing between them. Sometimes one will be tired and the other has to do more work, or one will fall and the other has to help the other up. At other times they're out of sync, there are obstacles to conquer together, and so on.

What do you imagine are potential problems that could come up in a marriage?

Even though your guys aren't married, they've certainly observed others who are and will be able to come up with a good list. Feel free to toss in some observations of your own, too.

Now, what if the partners weren't facing the same direction? How much more difficult would that be?

Of course it will be more of a challenge. Encourage guys to think about this, though. In what ways might couples "face opposite directions"? By having different backgrounds? By having experienced different upbringings? By having grown up in different cultures? These are all going to make for some challenges, but there is one that's a biggie—a different faith.

Read this verse aloud or have one of the guys read it:

 "Don't team up with those who are unbelievers. How can righteousness be a partner with wickedness? How can light live with darkness? What harmony can there be between Christ and the devil? How can a believer be a partner with an unbeliever?" (2 Corinthians 6:14-15)

What do you think this means? Do you think this verse is true? Why or why not?

If you married a girl who was not a Christian, how is that similar to running a three-legged race, but facing opposite directions? How might you and your wife have different perspectives on things?

Take your time here. See what they come up with, and then try to work in some of the points below. The perspectives of Christians and non-Christians on some matters will be very similar. On others…not so much. See what issues the guys can come up with that could be a problem. Some things you might mention:

Christians know they are accountable to God and must live by the principles of God's Word—which include a lot about how to be a great mate. They can't just simply do as they please or react as they feel. God is their boss.

Non-Christians live as if they're accountable only to themselves. They believe they have the right to do as they please. They are often guided by their own feelings—and feelings can change—especially in a marriage.

What is the significance of a non-Christian having a sin nature, even though she may be the nicest, sweetest girl you've ever met?

The sin nature can be a fooler. Inside this sweet girl is a natural tendency toward selfishness, jealousy, anger, and so on. See Galatians 5:19-21.

What does the non-Christian not have because she doesn't have the Holy Spirit? And how important are these things to a good marriage?

A non-Christian doesn't have the Holy Spirit helping her, teaching her, and cultivating fruits in her like love, joy, peace, patience, kindness, goodness, faithfulness, gentleness, and self control (Galatians 5:22-23).

So a few ways in which Christians and non-Christians are facing in opposite directions are:

- their perspective on life, and

- the presence of the Holy Spirit.

Listen to this verse:

 "The sinful nature wants to do evil, which is just the opposite of what the Spirit wants. And the Spirit gives us desires that are the opposite of what the sinful nature desires. These two forces are constantly fighting each other, so you are not free to carry out your good intentions" (Galatians 5:17).

The verse speaks of the fight within a Christian between his old nature and the Holy Spirit. Doesn't it make sense that there would be a fundamental conflict if you had the Holy Spirit and your wife didn't?

But what if you and the nonbelieving girl both seem to be on the same page totally. How can that go wrong?

We all change. Five or six years ago you probably hated girls. Now you can't stop thinking about them. If we're letting the Holy Spirit guide our lives (Galatians 5:16), we will change. Let me read part of Galatians 5:17 to you again. Listen for how your desires will change.

 "And the Spirit gives us desires that are the opposite of what the sinful nature desires."

What does this say about our desires and the desires of a non-Christian?

Unless the Christian is resisting the Spirit, the desires of a Christian and a non-Christian will be moving in *opposite* directions. God gives us new desires.

If it is true that we will be growing apart, how good can that marriage really be?

Now, if you were dating a girl who didn't believe in Jesus but was really sweet, do you think you might have a hard time believing either of you will change? Why or why not?

How might the phrase "love is blind" come into play in this case?

What does that tell you about the danger of even *dating* a non-Christian?

The road to marriage starts on a casual date. A girl can melt your heart, Christian or not. Before you know it, you're in love—and potentially headed for heartache.

What about "missionary dating"? Maybe she'll become a Christian while we date—right?

Don't count on it. Even Solomon got spiritually sidetracked by women who didn't share his belief in God. Invite her to church. Stay in a group—but avoid dating. It's dangerous and more likely to change you than her.

Sum It Up

We need to make a choice. Will we trust God's Word that no matter how good a girl looks, if she isn't a committed follower of Christ it could be a dangerous and costly mistake to go out with her? What will that look like in our lives?

When is the best time to make a decision about whether you should date a girl who isn't a committed follower of Christ? Now, when you aren't dating her—or after you've gone out on a few dates with her? Explain your answer.

Proverbs 4:25-27 says, "Look straight ahead, and fix your eyes on what lies before you. Mark out a straight path for your feet; stay on the safe path. Don't get sidetracked; keep your feet from following evil."

What do you think this means related to our topic?

Guys, think about when you were tied together for the race. Whether you were both facing forward, or one was forward and the other backward, was there any difference in how physically close you were to each other at that moment before the race started?

They will admit they were just as close physically.

| The unoffical record in 100m three-lagged race with a time of 12.8 sec. was set by two Germans named Ernst Schultze and Emil Wernicke. |

This is the deceptive thing about dating a girl who isn't a follower of Christ. You feel like you couldn't possibly be closer. You may be right. But you need to trust God that this is not his plan. You'll be going in opposite directions. You'll both begin to see things quite differently from each other over time.

TIP:
Gather all your obstacle course items...and then put them away!

Like running the obstacle course with one of you facing backward, your marriage will be much more difficult for you. You certainly won't have the kind of marriage God intended.

I want to challenge you to make a commitment to dating only a girl who is a dedicated follower of Christ. Anything less is living dangerously. The prize won't be a million bucks like in the imaginary marathon I talked about earlier, but it will be a marriage any guy would pay a million bucks to get.

|◯| **E-MAIL REMINDER (2-3 DAYS LATER)**

- Recap the main points (in just a few lines) of the importance of dating/marrying only a dedicated follower of Christ.
- Encourage them to make a personal commitment to pursue or date only a dedicated Christian—to trust God with this. "Since we are living by the Spirit, let us follow the Spirit's leading in every part of our lives" (Galatians 5:25).
- Add a one-line teaser about next week's session.
- Attach digital photos.

END CHAPTER TWENTY

THEME
Choosing a date (and eventually a mate) based on her heart, and not just on her looks, is wise.

TITLE

Beauty Is a Beast

C | **21**

CHAPTER

RISK

LOW   MED   HI

● PREP

This session has the potential of being one of those gatherings the guys will always remember. It's an easy one to lead, but let me encourage you to put every bit of prayer and prep into it so that you achieve maximum impact.

Start by finding a used car lot you can bring the guys to. You may want to talk to the staff there ahead of time to make sure they're OK with you bringing a group of guys onto their lot to look at cars. (It's likely they'll love the idea—since a lot of the guys are in the age group of looking for a first car!) You'll also need a place to talk after your car lot exercise, and generally a fast-food place will work just fine.

SHOPPING LIST

- locate a local used car lot
- digital camera

● GETTING STARTED

Bring the guys to the used car lot, and explain that you're going to give them 15 minutes to select their dream car or truck. Price is no object, because you're not buying them anything. When the time is up, they're all to meet back with you. Then, one at a time, each of the guys will get a turn to take the whole group to the vehicle he's selected to explain exactly why he chose it.

You may want to coach the guys not to run around the lot or touch the cars so the sales staff doesn't get nervous. If a salesperson approaches, you might explain that each of the guys is pretending to pick his dream vehicle and that you're keeping an eye on them. If the guys aren't rowdy, you shouldn't have a problem. If you do this on a Sunday, many dealers are closed and you can avoid the questions.

Be sure to grab a picture of each guy with his car or truck as he explains to the group why he chose it. You'll probably hear "selling points" like these:

"I just really love the way this car looks. It has great-looking lines."

"I think it would feel so great to drive a car like this."

"I'd love to see the looks on the faces of my friends when they see me drive up in this."

"This car is so quick!"

After each of the guys has had a chance to share, head to the fast-food place.

● TAKE IT TO THE NEXT LEVEL

Once the guys have grabbed a snack and are sitting down, start tying this together.

When you guys shared why you liked the car or truck you chose, I heard a lot about how the car looked, how you'd feel driving it, how fun it was, or how jealous it would make your other friends. Some of you liked the way the car would handle or some of the features it had. Am I missing anything?

You're just setting things up right now. If one of the guys mentioned the need to make sure the car is mechanically sound, that's great. Then springboard off that by pointing out that many guys wouldn't even give that a thought initially. If no one mentioned the mechanical end of things, start moving in that direction.

If you were really choosing a vehicle—one that will last for a long time, one that will go the distance—getting a car or truck that looks nice is great, but it isn't nearly as important as how sound the car is mechanically. Would you agree with that or not?

A lot of your reasoning for choosing a vehicle back at the lot did boil down to surface stuff—how the car looked or how it made you feel.

In life, we can easily make some big decisions based on looks and feelings, too. Can somebody give me an example?

How about dating decisions? How do a lot of guys choose the girl they ask out, or the girl they'd *like* to ask out?

You're all guys—so what do guys look for in a girl?

Let them come up with a good list! It will be interesting to see what they're looking for. Encourage them to share why each of the things they're looking for is important.

It can be easy to focus on the "surface" things, can't it, like how the girl looks. Is that right or wrong? Can it get us in trouble? Why or why not?

The thing is, we can get so revved up by the way a girl looks and by thoughts about being with her, it can totally cloud our rational thinking. What do we need to consider about a girl once she turns our head?

You may start hearing some things dealing with her personality, her beliefs, and so on. This is good. Keep it going.

What types of things are important—what qualities should a girl have if you really want the relationship to last?

How important is her relationship with God and why?

Make them think. Listen for "stock" answers versus their sharing what they truly believe.

What about her level of commitment to God? How might that impact your relationship in the long run?

You could have a great discussion on this point alone. A strong commitment to God means she isn't governed solely by

| The first auto race in the United States took place in Evanston, Illinois, on November 28, 1895.

her own feelings. She recognizes she is under God's authority. If she follows God's guidelines, she'll be committed to her marriage someday, too.

As red-blooded guys, we can get wrapped up in thinking about sex. We think the girl who looks the hottest will give us the most satisfying sex in a marriage setting. And if the sex is great, the marriage is great. Right? The world's "great marriage formula" goes something like this: "One great-looking girl = great sex and happiness in marriage." Do you think that's true? Why or why not?

You may get a little uncomfortable asking this question. But here's the thing. We want to be relevant, and let's face it—guys often buy into this myth. We want to move them toward thinking a little deeper, and you're the one who they're looking to for some guidance.

The "formula" is a myth. When a woman is into herself, or if a couple fights all the time, they aren't going to have a great relationship. So if a couple doesn't have a great relationship, how good do you think the sex will really be?

We just want them to see the correlation here.

The real formula is a little different. "A man and woman who honor God in their hearts + dedicated work and commitment = a great relationship, which leads to great sex."

Do you believe good relationships take a lot of work? Do you have any examples of that? Do you believe some of that work means you have to put the needs of the other person above your own? Why or why not?

A woman with a heart that honors God is more likely to work at a relationship. Why? Because she's accountable to God and has a heart that's willing to put in effort to make her marriage the way God intended it to be.

So, how can we know a girl's heart?

Tough question. The guys may point out that you can watch how she acts, listen to what she says, and so on.

Who's the one who truly knows a girl's heart—or anyone's heart, for that matter?

It's an obvious question, so treat the guys like you know they know.

God knows everyone's heart. Now if he knows everybody's heart, what might be a good thing to do before you get all excited about the way a girl looks?

Ask God to lead you to make wise choices regarding the girl you date and eventually, the girl you marry.

If you want a car that will go the distance, you'd ask a mechanic's advice before making a decision on which one to purchase. We need to go to God like a "heavenly mechanic" and ask for his help, too. Ask him to reveal the girl's heart to you.

Let me share a couple of verses with you.

 "Charm is deceptive, and beauty does not last; but a woman who fears the Lord will be greatly praised" (Proverbs 31:30).

 "The Lord doesn't see things the way you see them. People judge by outward appearance, but the Lord looks at the heart" (1 Samuel 16:7b).

How do these verses apply to what we're talking about?

Sum It Up

When it came to you guys picking a car or truck, I didn't see a lot of concern about how the vehicle was mechanically. Nobody said, "This is the car I'd choose, but if I were really buying it, I'd want a mechanic to check it out first." Most of you got so wrapped up in the surface stuff that you took the mechanical end for granted. Maybe you just assumed the cars were as good under the hood as they appeared to look on the outside. That can be a costly mistake when buying a car.

When we fail to consider the heart of a girl we want to date and mainly get wrapped up with the surface stuff, like her looks, we're making a dangerous mistake. Does that make sense?

Don't beat this to death. We're just making sure everyone is tracking with you.

Now, if you see the value in looking for a girl who is serious about her relationship with God, what do you think *she* is looking for in a *guy*?

A lot of guys don't really think about this. They're only thinking about the girl for them—not about being the guy a girl is looking for. But it only makes sense that she is going to be looking beyond the surface and desiring a guy who is serious about his relationship with God.

So if you want a relationship with a Christian girl, what does that suggest you'd better be working on?

They need to work on their own walk. Ask God to make their heart like his. OK, you've given the guys a lot to think about. And you may have made some significant progress toward busting some myths about what makes for a happy marriage and great sex in marriage. Great job. You can build on this in the future, reminding them to ask God to work on their own hearts, and to reveal the hearts of the girls they're thinking of dating.

|▭| E-MAIL REMINDER (2-3 DAYS LATER)

- Encourage them to ask God to reveal a girl's heart before dating her.
- Remind them to ask God to give them a "tuneup" so they are becoming the kind of guy who a committed Christian girl would be interested in.
- Attach a digital picture of them with their dream car or truck.
- Give them a one-liner about next week's session, and encourage them to join you.

Reprinted and adapted from "Beauty Is a Beast" in *Mashed Potatoes, Paint Balls...and Other Indoor/Outdoor Devotionals You Can Do With Your Kids* by Tim Shoemaker. Copyright © 2002 by Tim Shoemaker. Used by permission of WingSpread Publishers, a division of Zur Ltd., 800-884-4571.

END CHAPTER TWENTY-ONE

TIP:
Remember to thank the person who let you hang out at the car lot without buying anything.

THEME

The devil is a master fisherman intent on setting his hooks in us. He uses all kinds of temptations, but guys will learn to recognize and avoid his bait.

C | 22

CHAPTER

TITLE
Lethal Lure

RISK

LOW   MED   HI

SHOPPING LIST

- fishing tackle box full of lures (If you don't have one, borrow one from someone at church or work.)

- fishing lure with a nasty hook to give each of the guys as a reminder

- digital camera

- optional: mounted fish to show as a visual

●PREP

This session is perfect to use on a camping trip, but it will work just as well wherever you normally meet with the guys. Prep is really easy for this one, but you'll need to work far enough ahead to line up two major things.

First, track down a fishing tackle box if you don't have one. Ask around—they're easier to find than you think. Try to find one that is chock-full of all kinds of lures. It's important that it has some big lures in it with lethal-looking hooks. If it doesn't, buy at least one for your devotion.

Second, pick up a lure for each of the guys to take home after the devotion as a visual reminder of the lesson. Try a sporting goods store or hit an Internet supplier. Look for closeouts, and get the biggest lures you can afford.

I found a simple metal lure that was painted red and white, with the triple-hook cluster dangling behind it. The brand was *Daredevle.* That seemed especially appropriate, and I made my purchase. The guys loved it.

●GETTING STARTED

Start by letting the guys explore the fishing tackle box. Have them lay a bunch of the lures out on a table for the visual effect. Now, ask them four big questions to set things up for a really important session about the dangers of temptation.

Why do you think a fisherman has so many different lures?

To attract different kinds of fish. Fishermen know what fish like. In case one kind doesn't work, there are others to try.

How can a fish be fooled by one of these lures with all the big hooks hanging off it?

They may say, "Because fish are stupid!" That's fine for now because we'll talk more about it later. Or maybe fish see only the lure and not the hook…who knows?

What does a fisherman do with the fish he catches?

Generally, he does one of three things:

- He eats the fish.

- He mounts the fish as a trophy (show it if you brought one).

- He throws the fish back.

Name one important character trait most fishermen possess, at least when it comes to fishing?

Patience.

● **TAKE IT TO THE NEXT LEVEL**

Send up a silent prayer for God to work and guide the discussion.

If you bought a lure for the guys, spread them out and have each guy pick one. Guys like fiddling with things while they talk, so this will work out well. This will be the same lure they take home and will be a reminder of the things you talked about the very first time they held it.

Important Note: *This is the part of the session that has a bit of danger potential.* The hooks are sharp, and they're hard to get out if guys get them stuck in their hands (or other body parts). If a guy gets a barb stuck in his hand, it's likely it will have to go all the way through and then the barb will have to be cut off before pulling it back out—you may want to mention this painful point to the guys before they start poking each other with the hooks.

After each of the guys has selected a lure, take a group picture with the guys each holding up their lure.

Christians have been called "fishers of men," but the devil and his demons are among the greatest fishermen of all time. List some of the bait the devil and his demons use to catch people.

Keep a list of their input.

Sometimes the bait is really subtle. How could a thing as simple as flattery be a deadly lure?

Flattery usually leads to pride. Pride has taken down more guys than pornography, for example. Pride gives birth to selfishness, arrogance, and hard hearts. Pride destroys relationships. It causes a guy to forget his dependence on God.

See if after sharing this example the guys can think of other subtle lures that have the potential to turn into something bigger.

The devil's tackle box isn't limited to bad things. Can you name any perfectly *good* things the devil can use to lure us away from God— things that might keep us from church, from spending time with God, or from taking time to think about spiritual things? How can they lure us away?

Jobs, sports, computer games, movies, music, and so on. Do note that these things themselves may be wonderful—it's only when they lure us away from God that they become bad.

A lure is something that looks like a good thing, but it isn't. A few minutes ago we talked about how fish could be fooled by some of these lures.

There are two main possibilities:

A. The fish don't see the hooks.

B. The fish think they can avoid them.

Let's look closer at these.

A. They don't see the hooks—maybe it's dark or the water is murky or the lure is moving quickly. How can that happen to us when it comes to the bait Satan is putting out for us?

That can happen if our sense of right and wrong gets a little murky, or if, in the rush of an "opportunity," we don't see the danger in some of the things we're pursuing.

Have one of the guys read Psalm 119, verses 9 and 105, aloud.

"How can a young person stay pure? By obeying your word."

"Your word is a lamp to guide my feet and a light for my path."

How can reading and obeying the Word help protect us from those lures?

B. Maybe some fish see the hooks, but they want the bait s-o-o-o bad they think they can avoid the hooks. How is this like or unlike us with the bait Satan is putting out for us?

Listen to James 1:14-15:

 "Temptation comes from our own desires, which entice us and drag us away. These desires give birth to sinful actions. And when sin is allowed to grow, it gives birth to death."

According to this verse, how can our own desires, the things we allow ourselves to hunger for, actually be dangerous and make us easier prey for the devil?

Have you ever deliberately ignored the hooks—felt you were an exception to the rule, figured you were entitled or that you wouldn't get caught when you satisfied some kind of appetite? If so, what happened?

If you have a story to share from your own life or of someone you know who ignored the lures of Satan and ended up in a bad place, now's the time to share it.

Sum It Up

Let's take a look at another Scripture passage. I'm going to read it, and then I'll want you to tell me what stood out to you.

 "For the Lord sees clearly what a man does, examining every path he takes. An evil man is held captive by his own sins; they are ropes that catch and hold him. He will die for lack of self-control; he will be lost because of his great foolishness" (Proverbs 5:21-23).

I The Chinese and Egyptians used fishing rods, hooks, and lines as early as 2,000 B.C. I

Tell me what you heard here.

Be sure they picked out these things:

- We do it to ourselves.

- We don't sin and walk away. We're captive in a real sense. Like a fish on a line, sin holds us captive. And often our minds. We *think* we're getting away with it—that we're free. We can walk away any time we want, right? We're just not ready to walk away, that's all. Welcome to Alcatraz. The guys need to wake up and see this self-deception for what it is.

- The stakes are high. This is life-and-death stuff. How we handle temptation makes the difference between a life that is rewarding or one that is full of regrets.

Can you imagine the fear a fish may feel when it realizes it's hooked? Here's one even scarier: taking the bait to do something wrong—feeling the pain of the hooks and knowing the devil or one of his demons is on the other end of the line. That's pure terror.

And like a fisherman, what does the devil or a demon do with the guys they catch?

- Devour them.

- Mount them—hold them up for everyone to see. "Look at this Christian. Guess what I caught him doing!"

Unlike a fisherman, what's one thing the forces of evil generally won't do with their catch?

Let them off the "hook" and throw them back.

Often people like to paint the Bible or Christianity as a restrictive life of "do's and don'ts." That isn't the case at all. God wants to protect us from the traps and hooks of the devil and his demons. How can God's guidance protect us?

I'm praying that you'll "look for the hook" when some bait is reeled past you. I'm asking God to help you avoid it and run the other way.

Read or have one of the guys read 1 Corinthians 6:18.

 "Run from sexual sin! No other sin so clearly affects the body as this one does. For sexual immorality is a sin against your own body."

For some, you need to do some talking to God. You're hooked on sin of some kind, whether you're ready to admit that or not. He is the only one who can cut the line. Go to him. Ask for his help. And don't delay. You can fight and struggle on your own like a fish on the line. All it's going to do is wear you down and make it easier for the devil to reel you in.

And I want to be there to help you, too. If you want to see me privately or talk sometime this week, let me know.

I want each of you to take the lure home. Put it on your desk, hang it on the wall, or take the hooks off and use it on your key chain. Let it be a visual reminder of the need to watch out for the bait the devil wants to snare you with.

A fish that thinks this is lunch (hold up a lure) *becomes* lunch. It's the same with us.

TIP:
Be sure lures are put away so no one gets painfully hooked.

Unfortunately, there is much more you could say. Realistically, you may want to follow this up with some one-on-one time with the guys. It's likely one or more of the guys are squirming right now. For some, the hooks are set deep, and they're going to need help.

Even though you asked them to talk to you if they want, don't think that will happen easily. The devil is going to yank that pole and make it hard for them to come to you. Pray about it and seek *them* out this week.

Additional Scriptures: James 1:12-17; 1 Corinthians 6:18-20.

⌷ E-MAIL REMINDER (2-3 DAYS LATER)

- Send a few short sentences to remind them about avoiding the bait.
- Maybe add your cellphone number and invite them to call you anytime—or set up a time to meet with each guy this week for a soft drink.
- Give them a teaser about next week's session.
- Attach a digital photo of the group holding up the lures.

Reprinted and adapted from "Fishing Lesson" in *Smashed Tomatoes, Bottle Rockets...and Other Outdoor Devotionals You Can Do With Your Kids* by Tim Shoemaker. Copyright © 2001 by Tim Shoemaker. Used by permission of WingSpread Publishers, a division of Zur Ltd., 800-884-4571.

END CHAPTER TWENTY-TWO

THEME

Guys will learn to take preventative measures *now* to avoid getting "burned" by temptation.

TITLE

Fireproof

●PREP

This session follows "Lethal Lure" in the book. While you can do these sessions in any order, there is a certain amount of logic to following "Lethal Lure" with "Fireproof." In "Lethal Lure," the guys saw how deadly it can be to fall to temptation. In "Fireproof," they'll be looking at ways to protect themselves against temptation.

I ordered the alum powder from a local pharmacy. I intended to get potassium aluminum sulfate, but what came in was ammonium alum. It came in 4-ounce bottles, and I ordered four of them. The powder was cheap, about $3 per bottle. You'll use one of the bottles for testing this ahead of time.

Mix one of the 4-ounce bottles with 1/2 cup of water. Cut the sleeves off a T-shirt. Take a permanent marker and mark one sleeve as "normal" and the other as "fire retardant." **Wearing safety goggles and gloves,** saturate the fire retardant sleeve in the solution, wring out any excess, and dry with a portable hair blow dryer. (Of course, you can just wait for it to dry...but aren't you interested to see what's going to happen?)

Once it's dry, you're ready to test this. Since you're working with fire, **plan to do this outside with a bucket of water or a hose handy.** It's a good idea to have someone else around to assist.

RISK

LOW   MED   HI

SHOPPING LIST

• alum powder—at least 4 ounces (ammonium alum or potassium aluminum sulfate)

• *gloves and protective eyewear* when mixing alum powder

• old T-shirt to test the fire-retarding process

• long item such as stick or fireplace poker to hold burning T-shirt

• scissors

• portable hair blow dryer

• stopwatch or watch with a second hand

• lighter

• permanent marker

• bucket of water or hose nearby ready to use

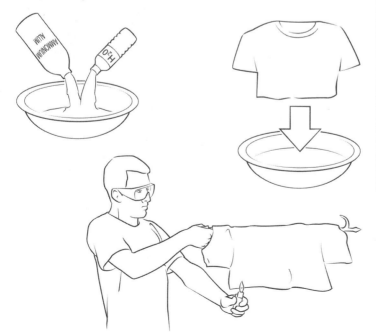

I burned the normal sleeve first by sliding it over the end of a fireplace poker and using the lighter. Take careful note how close you hold the flame so you can repeat it exactly the same way with the fire retardant sleeve. Time it to see how long it takes for the sleeve to totally burn up.

Next, I repeated the procedure with the fire retardant sleeve. The sleeve took longer to ignite, and once it did, it burned much slower. In fact, the burning sleeve extinguished itself before the fire totally consumed it. While that was impressive, it certainly wasn't *fireproof.* The T-shirt still burned—just not as fast or as extensively.

Finally, test it one more time by cutting off another hunk of the original T-shirt and soaking it in water. While still dripping wet, apply the fire. This is cheap and super effective. If you don't want to do the whole alum thing, you can probably get by with just soaking the shirt with water. In the devotion below, we'll do it all three ways.

● GETTING STARTED

Get the guys together and tell them about the solution you tested to make cloth fire-retardant. Tell them right upfront that it didn't make the cloth totally fireproof. You never know what the guys may try if you don't make that clear.

You may want to have one of the guys **wear the goggles and gloves** and mix the alum solution. Have a couple of other guys cut the sleeves off a T-shirt and mark them as you did in your practice session. Go through the procedure of drying, burning, timing, and noting observations just as you did in your trial run. You should be able to get every guy involved in some step along the way—and don't forget to grab some pictures while they're burning the sleeves.

Once you've tested both sleeves, be sure the sleeves are totally extinguished with water.

Now cut one more piece of the T-shirt, soak it in water, and have the guys try to ignite it while it's dripping wet. Take note that it won't ignite, and then move on. **To be on the safe side, collect the scissors and lighter,** and then get the guys together to talk about the little experiment.

● TAKE IT TO THE NEXT LEVEL

If you did "Lethal Lure" last week, remind them of how you learned that the devil and his demons would like to catch and destroy us by running various temptations by us.

Today we want to talk about how to avoid getting *burned* by temptation. We treated the cloth to make it more resistant to fire. Can you list some things we can do to make ourselves more resistant to temptation?

Think about something that's a temptation to you. What are basic things you can do ahead of time, when you aren't being tempted, to make the temptation less powerful or not an issue at all?

Why don't we *always* do those things?

Have you ever tried to get as close to a temptation as you could without actually giving in to the temptation? If so, what usually happens?

Guys may not be willing to share this aloud, but let them think on it for a moment.

Have you ever felt deep down that you'd like to get so close to the temptation that you do fall? Secretly, do you want the temptation bad enough to bring yourself to a point of no return?

You may not get a verbal response, but all the guys have been there.

Listen to James 1:14-15:

 "Temptation comes from our own desires, which entice us and drag us away. These desires give birth to sinful actions. And when sin is allowed to grow, it gives birth to death."

Put this verse into your own words. What does it mean to you?

According to this verse, if we don't deal with our desires, we're going to get burned. Many times this leads to an inner conflict. We want to avoid falling to temptation, yet we still secretly want it. We think about it, wishing there was a way to have it. This is a divided heart.

2 Chronicles 12 talks about King Rehoboam's failure. Verse 14 traces it down to his heart. "But he was an evil king, for he did not seek the Lord with all his heart."

A divided heart will generally lead to failure. If we allow ourselves to *want* something bad enough, even though we believe it's wrong, we'll likely find a way to get it—and the forces of evil are happy to help. Often they reveal a way within our power to satisfy the need—*now.*

Does anybody want to share an example of when something like this happened to you or someone you know?

If not, do you have an example you can share?

It's a whole lot easier to fall to temptation when you're standing on the edge peering into it. Isn't that why we fall so often? We allow ourselves to get too close instead of seeing how far away we can stay from it.

Relate this to the fire and the T-shirt. How is putting the "fireproof" that doesn't really completely stop the fire on a T-shirt like playing around with temptation—getting close to whatever is wrong?

Resisting temptation isn't about missing a lot of fun. It's about avoiding the consequences of that temptation. It's about protecting ourselves from hurt, pain, regret, and loss. Do you agree or disagree with that? Why?

Read the account of Joseph and Potiphar's wife in Genesis 39:8-12.

What did Joseph do?

- He said "no."

- He reviewed his biblical perspective of right and wrong.

- He avoided going near the temptation.

Joseph had decided in advance he'd do things God's way, and when a shortcut to satisfaction presented itself, he effectively resisted it.

Sometimes temptation is unavoidable. It's right in our path. But that doesn't mean we have to fall. How did Joseph resist sexual temptation in Genesis 39:12?

He "tore himself away" and he "ran from the house."

Do you think it was easy for Joseph? Why or why not?

He "tore" himself away. That doesn't sound easy. It took effort.

He *distanced* himself from the danger as quickly as he could. How important was it that he ran?

How can we literally run from temptation?

Sum It Up

We went to a lot of time and trouble to try to make the cloth fireproof with that solution, with only marginal results. Soaking it with water was even more effective, and easier. There are things we can do to protect ourselves from temptation. Some will take more effort than others. We talked about that before, but let's review them and add more.

What are basic things we can do to keep from falling and getting hurt by temptation?

Ideas the guys might share or that you can touch on are:

- Settle the issue in your mind ahead of time—end the divided heart.

- Commit to integrity like Joseph—trust God to reward you *in his time.*

- Avoid things, places, friends, and so on that will make resisting tougher.

- Set up accountability partners, talk with parents, or get professional help.

- Ask God for his help like Jesus taught in Matthew 6:13.

I Alum is used to make foamite which is used in many fire extinguishers for chemical and oil fires. I

- Know what the Bible says so you can resist temptation like Jesus.
- Run like Joseph did when temptation crosses your path.

If we don't get away from the temptation quickly, it may consume us, too, no matter how good our intentions are.

For some, the temptation has reached more of an addiction proportion. Tearing away for good seems impossible, or something you're not quite ready to try.

TIP:
Be sure flames are all out and all chemicals are put away.

God can help. The Bible tells us he sets prisoners free (Psalm 146:7). Pray that he will give you new desires.

 "Take delight in the Lord, and he will give you your heart's desires. Commit everything you do to the Lord. Trust him, and he will help you" (Psalm 37:4-5).

Don't forget to bring it to God and ask for his help.

 "And don't let us yield to temptation, but rescue us from the evil one" (Matthew 6:13).

Remember, there isn't a guy in the group that hasn't failed in some way at some time. They may be convicted of that right now. This might be a good time to remind them of God's forgiveness in 1 John 1:9.

E-MAIL REMINDER (2-3 DAYS LATER)

- Send a brief sum-up of the basic methods to resist temptation and how it all starts in their hearts.
- If you didn't set up a time to get together with each guy individually last week, do it now.
- Give a one-line teaser about next week's session.
- Attach a picture.

END CHAPTER TWENTY-THREE

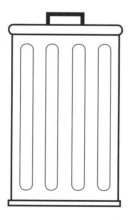

THEME
Pornography is lethal to God's plan for good, pure sex.

TITLE
Sugar Substitute

WARNING
! SULFURIC ACID !

C | 24
CHAPTER

PREP

The effect of sulfuric acid on sugar is extraordinary, making this an excellent visual for an essential topic. Since you'll be working with a poisonous chemical that can cause burns, you may consider passing this one by because of the potential danger. Don't. That would be infinitely more dangerous because the guys *desperately* need to hear this.

Pornography is a monster. This vicious demon tears men and marriages apart—probably much more than we know. The most important preparation you can do for this session will be on your knees. Pray for the guys—some of whom have already been lured into the prison of pornography. Maybe you've struggled with it, too—or continue to struggle. Pornography doesn't release its prisoners easily. I believe only God can rescue a guy from porn's grip.

Because ***sulfuric acid is a dangerous chemical,*** it's not available to everyone. But it is used in some drain openers. Rooto Professional Drain Opener is concentrated sulfuric acid and works perfectly. It's available at most hardware stores, but you still may have to show identification and sign your name before purchasing this.

Do this activity outside. The chemical reaction emits *strong odors.* Follow all safety instructions on the bottle—like keep it away from kids, clothing, skin, and eyes. *Wear gloves, eye protection, and have water in a bucket or a running hose nearby.*

- Fill the glass about half full with sugar.
- Pour a modest amount of sulfuric acid into the glass.
- Stir immediately with the pencil. Add sulfuric acid as needed. Mix thoroughly to paste or pudding consistency.
- Remove the pencil, step back, and observe.

The sugar quickly darkens to brown and then black. The tarlike solution starts to boil, and wisps of steam escape as a column of carbon rises above the glass. Spectacular, isn't it? A perfect illustration of the acid effect that pornography has on God's plan for sex.

- Let the glass cool before handling it.

RISK

LOW MED **HI**

SHOPPING LIST

- *safety goggles for each of the guys*
- *chemical-resistant gloves for each guy*
- clear drinking glass (You'll throw this away at the end, so don't use a good one.)
- 5-pound bag of granulated sugar
- sulfuric acid (see "Prep")
- stir stick (An unsharpened pencil works fine.)
- sugar packets—like you'd get at a restaurant (1 for each guy)
- digital camera

TIP:
Sulfuric acid is corrosive and will burn skin (or other things that it gets on). Use extreme caution when handling it, and supervise teens closely if you let them do the mixing. And be sure to wear chemical-resistant gloves when you do!

Also be sure to *do this activity outside* to be sure any fumes aren't captured indoors.

The glass you use for this activity may break, and will be hot to the touch. Let it cool when you're done, and then you can throw the whole thing away.

● **GETTING STARTED**

Before the demonstration, pull out some sugar and give everyone a taste while you talk.

This is pure sugar. What do you like that has sugar in it?

What foods that you've heard about kind of surprise you that sugar has been added for taste?

For example, most ketchup has sugar in it. It's added to a lot of foods!

What foods that have sugar would taste terrible if the sugar were left out?

Now be sure you move outside for the experiment!

Now, let's see what happens to this pure sugar when I add acid to it.

Be sure the guys are wearing safety goggles and gloves before they participate in any way. Run through the demonstration just the way you practiced it earlier. Be sure to securely screw the cap back on the sulfuric acid and put it away after every use. Grab photos of the sugar after it has finished rising.

Keep the bag of pure sugar and the mutated sugar column with you during the discussion time.

● **TAKE IT TO THE NEXT LEVEL**

I'd like you to think of the bag of pure sugar here as sex. Good, clean sex the way God created it—to be enjoyed by a man and woman committed to each other in marriage. A lot of times sex is portrayed as being dirty—but God created it as a beautiful expression of love between a married couple.

The sulfuric acid represents pornography and its effect on sex.

First, how many of you have friends or know guys who have looked at some form of pornography?

Notice, you're not asking how many of *them* have seen it.

How many of you know guys who seem to be hooked on it?

We've all heard that pornography is wrong, but I also want you to understand how porn will hurt you and those you love. I hope to be able to show you how it will destroy the very things you want most.

OK. A few minutes ago we mentioned some of the benefits of pure sugar: how it makes plain things much more appetizing, how it's so good, and so on. Now, let's relate it to sex. What do you think were God's two big reasons for inventing sex?

- to populate the earth
- to draw a man and wife together in a closeness unequaled by anything else

Let's zero in on how God intended sex to sweeten marriage. Besides producing children, how do you think sex benefits a guy and his wife in marriage?

Give them a moment here—but not uncomfortably long. They're all thinking, but they may not be quite willing to share. It's an uncomfortable topic! Here are some ideas they might come up with or ones you might suggest:

- It strengthens the two in a physical and emotional bond.
- It promotes trust between the two.
- It rekindles passionate love.
- It reminds couples how much they need each other.
- It tends to make the worries, fears, and problems of the day melt away. It makes a hard day bearable in light of the anticipation of being together.
- Oh, and it feels good, too. It's a reward.

That's how God designed sex—with *lots* of benefits.

Rank this next question from 1 to 10, with 1 being least important and 10 being extremely important. How important would you say good, frequent, and passionate sex is to a great marriage?

OK. Now if good sex is *that* important, *that* essential, and *that* beneficial to a marriage, should we be surprised that the devil would like to mess that up? Why or why not?

One of the ways the devil messes up good sex in a marriage is through pornography. Not just when guys look at porn when

I Pure undiluted sulfuric acid is not encountered on earth. I

they're married, but now—at your age. How can looking at porn now mess up your chances for good sex in marriage?

You may get insightful input, or you may not. Help them out.

- *Porn gives false expectations.* Porn promotes selfish sex. Porn portrays a false image of what sex will be like when you're married. When sex isn't like what you've been led to expect, it will lead to problems in your marriage.

- *Porn twists your tastes.* When you love your wife, sex is about expressing true love. Porn is about unleashing pure lust. Big difference. Porn will subtly lead you away from sex between one man and one woman committed to each other in marriage. You will get appetites for things you never would have imagined otherwise.

- *Porn separates you from the real world.* Married guys addicted to porn often prefer the imaginary to the real. They'll exchange a chance for sex with their wife for a chance to watch porn. It's like going to a restaurant when you're hungry. Can you imagine just looking at the pictures on the menu instead of ordering something? That's what porn will do to you.

- *Porn will push you to live out your fantasies.* Guys into porn need more and more to satisfy them, and eventually they'll look for other ways to fulfill their sexual fantasies. This is deadly, lethal—whether a guy's married or not.

- *Porn is addicting.* If you're into it now, chances are extremely high you'll still be involved in it when you're married. Fast-forward ahead to when you're married to a girl you totally love. A girl you've committed your life to. A girl you'd die for. If you're into porn after you're married, here's how your wife will interpret your actions:

  - "I can never satisfy him. I can never be enough." *No matter how hard she might try to please you, you'll still be addicted to pornography. As a result, she may shy away from sex or give up, feeling like she can't measure up. Think about this question. How devastating to your marriage would it be if your wife stops wanting to have sex?*

  - "My body isn't good enough." *The fact that you look at other women tells your wife she isn't pretty enough. That leads to feelings of failure and low self-esteem. It's truly like she's getting emotionally beat up—and instead of helping her, you're the one hitting her.*

  - "I can never trust him." *Because you're addicted, you'll go back to the porn. She'll lose trust and respect for you. What do you think that does for your sex life with her?*

There's much more you could say. You can be fairly certain some of the guys are already into porn. Pray that the Holy Spirit speaks to their hearts and helps them.

Sex is one of God's greatest inventions. The forces of darkness want to take this good thing and turn it into something twisted and ugly.

Hold up the burnt sugar in the cup. Ask the guys to consider how adding one small ingredient changed the sugar.

TIP:
Be very careful disposing of the items from this experiment.

Pornography will change you and in many ways ruin sex for you. Instead of sugar, you'll get this column of carbon here. Would any of you want to sprinkle some of this on your cereal in the morning?

Guys, I'm pleading with you to guard yourselves in this area. Like sulfuric acid on sugar, porn will burn you badly. And it doesn't take much to do it.

Can any of you change this burnt sugar back to its original, pure form?

No. Only God can do something like that.

Maybe some of you have already dabbled in porn. You may be addicted and don't know it yet. Ask God to help you, and stay away from it from now on. Jesus can set captives free. Don't be afraid to ask for help from your parents or me.

If you indulge in porn, you can't avoid its consequences. So don't mess with it. It's poison. Just like the warning label on this bottle of sulfuric acid warns of the danger of being burned or poisoned, so I'm warning you that porn can be lethal.

Have one of the guys read this verse aloud:

 "So listen to me, my sons, and pay attention to my words. Don't let your hearts stray away toward her. Don't wander down her wayward path. For she has been the ruin of many; many men have been her victims. Her house is the road to the grave. Her bedroom is the den of death" (Proverbs 7:24-27).

Sex in marriage can be very sweet. It's worth waiting for—and worth protecting. Porn makes a poor sugar substitute.

Give each guy a sugar packet to keep in his backpack or room as a reminder to protect the "sugar" in their future by avoiding all types of pornography from this point on.

Additional Scriptures: Proverbs 4:14-15; 5:3-13, 20-23; 6:25-26; Galatians 5:16-17.

|▢| E-MAIL REMINDER (2-3 DAYS LATER)

- Encourage guys to avoid porn, or get help if they're already involved in it.
- Add a one-line teaser about next week's session, encouraging them to attend.
- Attach a digital photo.

END CHAPTER TWENTY-FOUR

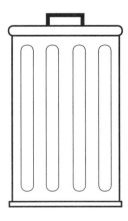

Conversions and Equivalents Charts

Length

When you know:	If you multiply by:	You can find:
inches	25	millimeters
inches	2.5	centimeters
feet	30	centimeters
yards	0.9	meters
miles	1.6	kilometers
millimeters	0.04	inches
centimeters	0.4	inches
meters	3.3	feet
meters	1.1	yards
kilometers	0.6	miles

Volume

When you know:	If you multiply by:	You can find:
teaspoons	4.9	milliliters
tablespoons	14.8	milliliters
fluid ounces	29.6	milliliters
cups	0.24	liters
pints	0.47	liters
quarts	0.95	liters
gallons	3.79	liters
milliliters	0.03	fluid ounces
liters	4.22	cups
liters	2.11	pints
liters	1.06	quarts
liters	0.26	gallons

Weight

When you know:	If you multiply by:	You can find:
ounces	28.4	grams
pounds	0.45	kilograms
grams	0.035	ounces
kilograms	2.2	pounds

Metric Equivalents Linear Weight

U.S.	Metric	U.S.	Metric
1/8 in	3 mm	1/4 oz	7 g
1/4 in	6 mm	1/2 oz	14 g
1/2 in	1.3 cm	3/4 oz	21 g
3/4 in	1.9 cm	1 oz	28 g
1 in	2.5 cm	8 oz (1/2 lb)	225 g
6 in	15 cm	12 oz (3/4 lb)	341 g
12 in (1 ft)	30 cm	16 oz (1 lb)	454 g
39 in	1 m	35 oz (2.2 lb)	1 kg

---

mm = millimeter
cm = centimeter
m = meter
in = inch
ft = foot

ml = milliliter
l = liter
tsp = teaspoon
tbsp = tablespoon
oz = ounce

fl oz = fluid ounce
qt = quart
gal = gallon
g = gram
kg = kilogram

lb = pound
C = celsius
F = fahrenheit

Temperature

U.S.	Metric
0°F (freezer temperature)	-18°C
32°F (water freezes)	0°C
98.6°F	37°C
180°F (water simmers*)	82°C
212°F (water boils*)	100°C
250°F (low oven)	120°C
350°F (moderate oven)	175°C
425°F (hot oven)	220°C
500°F (very hot oven)	260°C

* 1 tablespoon (tbsp) = 3 teaspoons (tsp)
* 1/16 cup (c) = 1 tablespoon
* 1/8 cup = 2 tablespoons
* 1/6 cup = 2 tablespoons + 2 teaspoons
* 1/4 cup = 4 tablespoons
* 1/3 cup = 5 tablespoons + 1 teaspoon
* 3/8 cup = 6 tablespoons
* 1/2 cup = 8 tablespoons
* 2/3 cup = 10 tablespoons + 2 teaspoons
* 3/4 cup = 12 tablespoons
* 1 cup = 48 teaspoons
* 1 cup= 16 tablespoons
* 8 fluid ounces (fl oz) = 1 cup
* 1 pint (pt) = 2 cups
* 1 quart (qt) = 2 pints
* 4 cups = 1 quart
* 1 gallon (gal) = 4 quarts
* 16 ounces (oz) = 1 pound (lb)
* 1 milliliter (ml) = 1 cubic centimeter (cc)
* 1 inch (in) = 2.54 centimeters (cm)

Dangerous Devotions in Action

Dangerous Devotions in Action